Poverty and Expectation in the Gospels

LONDON
SPCK

First published 1980
SPCK
Holy Trinity Church
Marylebone Road
London NW1 4DU

Filmset in Great Britain by
Northumberland Press Ltd, Gateshead, Tyne and Wear
Printed by
Fletcher and Son Ltd, Norwich

ISBN 0 281 03706 x

Contents

Preface

It was in 1965 that I first became interested in the diverse attitudes to poverty and riches in the period of the New Testament. The pages which follow focus especially on the gospels, and aim to discuss all the main passages on the subject in the Synoptic Gospels in the light of modern methods of New Testament study. Readers will notice that I have paid some attention to the question of the social and economic background of the gospels, as well as to more familiar questions of redaction, source, and form criticism. Although this is chiefly a historical study, I have concluded with reflections on the use made of the New Testament evidence in some recent pronouncements on social ethics. It is not an easy task to turn from an ancient text to problems of the present, and I have tried to indicate some of the factors which should be remembered when modern readers consult the gospels with contemporary problems in mind. The gospels have had such a formative influence on the beliefs and attitudes of Western civilization that they deserve careful and considered study.

This book does, in fact, represent my second thoughts on attitudes to poverty and riches in the gospels. An earlier and much longer study of this theme in the whole New Testament period was written in 1971 as an M.Litt. thesis under the shrewd eye of Professor K. Grayston of Bristol University. I wish to express my gratitude to him, and to my colleagues at Wells in the period 1966–71 where the combination of smooth organization and lively academic debate made writing and research not only possible but also a delight. I am also grateful to Professor J. McIntyre whose timely and helpful advice in 1976 encouraged me to select and rewrite the earlier material. I knew then that my interests were moving in a more philosophical direction, and that this was the time to rewrite and publish some of my earlier work. In 1977 a period of sabbatical leave from my present post in Edinburgh University enabled me to do much of the rewriting in Tübingen. There I was able to consult Professor M. Hengel, to use the excellent libraries, and to stay at the Stift. The latter was a good place to visit, with an atmosphere conducive to sustained writing, and the present book is the result.

My wife and children, my friends, colleagues, and acquaintances have all been subjected to the demands of this work for a long time. I cannot name all who have responded heroically to barrages of questions, expressions of hopeless puzzlement, or other requests for help. I just hope that I have not abused too badly their patience and acute and helpful contributions. I do wish to express particular thanks to my wife for her help with the script, to Patricia Donoghue and to Gill Ellis who typed successive drafts, and to the Editor and staff of SPCK for their skill in completing the task.

Edinburgh DAVID L. MEALAND
February 1979

ACKNOWLEDGEMENTS

Thanks are due for permission to quote from copyright sources:

SCM Press Ltd: *The Sayings of Jesus* by T. W. Manson. (U.S. rights by permission of Wm. B. Eerdmans Publishing Co.)

Quotations from the Revised Standard Version of the Bible, copyrighted 1946 and 1952 by the Division of Christian Education of the National Council of the Churches of Christ in the U.S.A. are used by permission.

Abbreviations

The following abbreviations are used throughout the book:

AGJU	Arbeiten zur Geschichte des antiken Judentums und des Urchristentums
BDB	F. Brown, S. R. Driver, and C. A. Briggs, *Hebrew and English Lexicon of the Old Testament*
BFCT	Beiträge zur Förderung christlicher Theologie
BHT	Beiträge zur historischen Theologie
BJRL	*Bulletin of the John Rylands Library*
BZ	*Biblische Zeitschrift*
BZNW	Beihefte zur Zeitschrift für die neutestamentliche Wissenschaft
CAH	*The Cambridge Ancient History*
CBQ	*Catholic Biblical Quarterly*
CSCO	Corpus Scriptorum Christianorum Orientalium
Ev T	*Evangelische Theologie*
Exp Tim	*Expository Times*
HTKNT	Herders theologischer Kommentar zum Neuen Testament
JBL	*Journal of Biblical Literature*
JESHO	*Journal of Economic and Social History of the Orient*
JTS	*Journal of Theological Studies*
KB	L. Koehler and W. Baumgartner, *Lexicon in Veteris Testamenti Libros*
LUA	Lunds Universitets Årsskrift
NEB	New English Bible
NF	Neutestamentliche Forschungen, Gütersloh
Nov T	*Novum Testamentum*
NTAbh	Neutestamentliche Abhandlungen
NTS	*New Testament Studies*
Preuss Jahrbuch	*Preussische Jahrbücher*, Berlin
RSV	Revised Standard Version of the Bible

Sci et Espr	*Science et Esprit*
SGKA	Studien zur Geschichte und Kultur des Altertums
SJT	*Scottish Journal of Theology*
STDJ	Studies on the texts of the desert of Judah
Str–B	(H. Strack and) P. Billerbeck *Kommentar zum Neuen Testament*
TDNT	*Theological Dictionary of the New Testament*
Theol Zeitschr (= *TZ*)	*Theologische Zeitschrift*
Th Ex Heute	Theologische Existenz Heute
VS	Verbum Salutis
Wiss Zeitschrift	*Wissenschaftliche Zeitschrift*, Berlin
WMANT	Wissenschaftliche Monographien zum Alten und Neuen Testament
WUNT	Wissenschaftliche Untersuchungen zum Neuen Testament
ZAW	*Zeitschrift für die alttestamentliche Wissenschaft*
ZKT	*Zeitschrift für katholische Theologie*
ZNW	*Zeitschrift für die neutestamentliche Wissenschaft*
ZTK	*Zeitschrift für Theologie und Kirche*

ONE

The Problem and the Economic Background to the Gospels

THE PROBLEM

In the Synoptic Gospels we read about those who are invited to leave all and to accompany Jesus. We hear blessings pronounced on 'the poor'. We encounter parables about people who give up everything in order to acquire buried treasure or a priceless pearl. The readers of the gospels are exhorted not to lay up treasure on earth, not to serve mammon, and not to be weighed down by cares about food and drink and clothes. We learn that when disciples were sent out they were told to travel with a minimum of impedimenta. If all this were not enough we also find parables which portray a rich man as either a fool (Luke 12.20) or a villain (Luke 16.19–31), and we read fierce denunciations of those who are wealthy and well fed (Luke 6.24–5). Luke also includes one of the most categorical statements of all: 'So then, every one of you who does not give up all his possessions cannot be my disciple.' (Luke 14.33.) [My trans.]

Eventually we shall need to ask how much of all this we are to assign to the evangelists, to the tradition, and to Jesus. That inquiry will occupy Chapters 2, 3, and 4 of this book. But before we undertake that task, a prior question needs to be investigated. That prior question concerns the economic background to the gospels. In Mark 6.8 Jesus tells his disciples to travel without food or copper coins, while Matthew 10.9 urges them to take no gold. Which is closer to the realities of life in first-century Galilee? When Matthew records a parable about unemployed labourers who wait for the chance to earn a denarius a day, we seem to be closer to the life of the villages. The view that the payment was a normal one is supported both by earlier texts (Tobit 5.14) and by later ones (Gen. R. 61). Yet Matthew also records a parable about a man who owed the enormous sum of ten thousand talents (Matt.

18.24). The sum is astronomical, representing the wages for 100 million working days, or fifty times the annual revenues paid by Galilee and Peraea to Herod Antipas (Jos. Ant. 17.318). We seem here to be in the realm of the oriental story teller. We must begin by exploring the economic life of Galilee and Judaea in the time of Jesus and his disciples. Then we can proceed to investigate the different emphases within the different gospels and try to place them in the context of the history of the time and the history of the tradition. The aim of this chapter is to take up the first of these tasks and offer an outline account of the economic background to the gospels.

THE ECONOMIC BACKGROUND

Agriculture

We are not concerned here with the large estates and slave labour common in Italy, nor the Roman city mobs dependent on the dole. The poverty and depopulation suffered by Greece are not our concern either, though the weak economic position of Paul's converts in Greek cities can be attested from his letters, and rural neglect in remote parts of Greece is vividly portrayed by Dio Chrysostom (Or. 7). Syria is closer to the area with which we are concerned. There irrigation was important; more corn was produced than in Palestine.[1] The province also produced beans and lupins, wine, olives, dates, and nuts. There were livestock, and also the growing of hemp and the extraction of minerals.

In Palestine the staple requirements of bread and fish, wine, and oil were in reasonable supply. In good years corn was exported, but rabbinic statements from after the fall of Jerusalem suggest that the yield then was five times the amount sown. Cattle were raised in the Trans-Jordanian grasslands, but meat was not staple. Some dates and pomegranates were produced. Wool and flax were also available.[2]

Josephus describes the fertility and productivity of Galilee. Wheat was produced and stored in Galilee. Dates, figs, walnuts, wine, and oil came from this region and, of course, fish.[3]

Industry and Trade

In Syria business was more profitable than farming.[4] The various crafts included the production of glass, papyrus, leather, cloth, dyes, and work in precious metals. The through trade from Babylonia to the coast was an important factor.

From Judaea we have information about the trades and crafts carried on in Jerusalem. The city was unfavourably placed for trade, but the Temple drew pilgrims and visitors to Jerusalem. Food and raw materials were imported from the locality and from further afield. In the city a variety of trades and crafts were practised. These included the sale of wool, and weaving and leather work. Building was an important industry and provided much employment. Timber was not plentiful, but stone was widely used. Luxury goods such as ointments and jewellery were also produced in the city.[5]

As for the crafts practised in Galilee, Hoehner is able to collect references to the export of salted fish, the weaving of linen, and the making of coarse cloth and mats. Jars for oil were also manufactured in the region. There were trade routes through the land, but agriculture seems to have been the main occupation of the inhabitants.[6] The chief commercial centres in the immediate neighbourhood were the cities along the Mediterranean coast of Palestine. 'Greek' and other pagan merchants traded there, although we do hear of Jewish-owned ships which attacked the sea routes during the great revolt.[7]

The People

In Syria, in addition to the peasants and urban proletariat we hear of doctors, lawyers and teachers, philosophers and historians.[8] There would also have been owners of large estates, and in the commercial centres and coastal cities wealthy merchants. The Gospel of Matthew and of Luke might well reflect the environment of hellenized cities like these, whereas the older traditions in the gospels are probably closer to the life of the early Church in Jerusalem or to the situation in Galilee during and after the ministry of Jesus.

The class structure of Judaea and especially of Jerusalem can be reconstructed to some extent from the ancient sources, though many gaps remain in the picture. It is estimated, for example, that Tiberius Alexander, who came from a wealthy Jewish family in Alexandria, earned some 100,000 sestertii officially as Roman governor of Judaea.[9] The revenues of Herod Agrippa during the period of his reign from A.D. 41 to A.D. 44 are given by Josephus as twelve million (drachmas).[10] This was several times the annual income Herod Antipas used to receive from Galilee and Peraea, but Herod Agrippa's territories were more extensive. We know less about the financial affairs of the aristocracy. The high priest and the families related to him are thought to have derived their wealth partly from large estates and partly from their duties in the Temple. The precise picture is far from clear, and even Jeremias, who offers pages of minute detail, has in the end to resort to surmise. He cites instances of the chief priests seizing the dues of their subordinates, and filling lucrative and influential posts in the Temple with members of their families, but concludes that their regular income came from the Temple treasury.[11] That great wealth was associated with the possession of extensive lands is more immediately evident, and the wealthy landowner was undoubtedly an important figure in first-century Palestine.[12] There also seem to have been a few rich merchants. The wealthy appear to have been a small group of people, mostly Sadducees, and well represented on the Sanhedrin.

Palestinian society fell largely into two groups: the small community of the rich and the great mass of the poor. Between these extremes there was perhaps a small middle class which did not have much influence. In his study of the class structure Kreissig includes here those with small farms, those engaged in handicrafts and local trade, chief tax collectors, and priests with lesser duties in the Temple. A further group includes tenant farmers, travelling workmen, pedlars, stallholders, tax collectors, physicians, 'Levites', household scribes, and wage earners with special skills. But classification by occupation is a very rough and ready guide.[13] Certain trades such as those of butchers, tanners, and people engaged in transport were despised. Such trades were either repugnant, or conducive to dishonesty, in the eyes of certain rabbis at least.[14] But the rabbis themselves should not be thought of as wealthy. They usually had to earn a living, and some were poor enough to do so as carpenters or day labourers. Hillel himself is said to have been very poor and to have earned only a victoriatus a day (half a denarius) as a day labourer (Joma 35b).

Among the great mass of the poor were those who worked as day labourers. Mishnaic rules give some insights into the nature of this employment. They forbid a man to hire labourers on the condition that a labourer's son shall glean behind him (Pea 5.6). Further rules cover the situation where a labourer is hired for the fig harvest, and he, or he and his family, are allowed to eat some of the crop (Maas. 2.7–8). The poorest sections of society certainly included widows, and those whom sickness or disability forced to depend on alms. Then there were also slaves, probably both Jewish and Gentile, although there may have been fewer Jewish slaves owned by Jews in the period we are considering.[15] The conditions of slaves varied considerably. Some had large responsibilities, and lacked the worries of day labourers uncertain about earning their bread. Others were undoubtedly exploited.

Information about large estates in Galilee in the first century is not easy to assemble in detail. A good deal of circumstantial evidence is available and points to the existence of estates owned by members of the Herodian family and officials of the Herods, and by the imperial family.[16] We hear of Crispus, who owned estates east of Jordan, and Josephus himself mentions land he owned in Judaea.[17] John of Gischala made large profits from transactions during the Jewish war, but is described by Josephus as having been 'poor at the outset'.[18] Parables in the gospels mention men with estates, but it is precisely the background to such teaching that we are investigating here. Philip, an official of Agrippa II, controlled villages at Gamala east of the Sea of Galilee (Jos. Vita 46–7). Three centuries earlier, a vineyard at Beth Anath in Galilee was inspected by an agent of the Ptolemaic administration. We also hear later from rabbinic times, the story of the owner of a Galilean vineyard who lived in Judaea and who struck a bargain with the owner of a Judaean vineyard who lived in Galilee.[19] The evidence for large estates in Galilee is not overwhelming, but we do have indications of their existence. We do not know much about the size of particular estates, or about the proportion of large and smaller holdings of land.

It is likely that in Galilee there were few people of moderate means between the influential rich and the great majority of the poor. Grant speaks of parcels of land passed down from the Maccabean allotments.[20] Later rabbinic stories tell of R. Johanan, who sold one or two pieces of land between Tiberias and Sepphoris in order to study the Torah. This sale left no provision for his old age.[21] If Zebedee had hired men, he may also have owned his fishing boat (Mark 1.20) but the gospels include such details only by accident. Hegesippus recounts that the grandsons of Judas the brother of Jesus between them owned land worth 9000 denarii. The land was thirty-nine plethra (about four hectares or nine acres) which they worked themselves (H.E. 3.20.1). One may have reservations about parts of Hegesippus's story but the size of the plot of land could well reflect the circumstances of the time. As for Palestinian house ownership, we have an occasional glimpse from the rules in the Mishnah. Some houses were rented (B.M. 8.6–9). Other houses were owned or part owned, as may be seen from the following legislation: 'If a house and an upper room belonging to two persons fall down, the two share in the wood and the stones and the earth; and they consider which stones were the more likely to have been broken. . . .' (B.M. 10.1, trans. Danby.) The descriptions of houses falling down or being broken into underscore the simplicity of the construction, as do the excavations of houses in Galilee.[22]

The Galilean poor probably closely resembled the majority of the poor in the rest of Palestine. Labourers were hired by the day and there were always situations where people could not get work or were unable to work. The day labourer's wage of a denarius a day had a purchasing power in terms of bread of something over six kilos in normal times. Out of that wage he would need to feed, clothe, and house himself and his family. Our information is limited, and the values of coins, weights, measures, and commodities varied from place to place, and from time to time, so only rough illustrations can be given. A loaf of bread, and either fruit or a dish of vegetables, was the diet of a labourer. A poor vagabond received bread worth one-twelfth of a denarius (just over 500 grams of bread). Mark, or his source, estimated 200 denarii were needed to supply bread to 5000 people (slightly more than 250 grams each).[23] Clothing was expensive. In Mishnaic times a cheap shirt or cloak cost about twelve denarii and a better one twice as much (Meilah 6.4). Heichelheim estimated the living costs of a single adult at about half a denarius[24] a day which gives some idea of the problems of those with larger families or earning smaller sums or with irregular employment.[25] The contrast of rich and poor in Galilee is well illustrated from the account in Josephus of the founding of Tiberias. It was constructed on the site of tombs and so was ritually impure. Herod Antipas built the houses and donated the land but had to populate it with people from Galilee and elsewhere, many of whom were without means, and some were former slaves (Jos. Ant. 18.37–8). During the revolt the ringleader of the sailors and the destitute looted Herod's former palace, tried to strip gold from the roof, and set the building on fire (Jos. Vita 66–7).

The gulf between rich and poor which we find in the gospels does reflect the circumstances of the time. In Galilee, in Judaea, and in Syria and further afield we find a similar polarization of society but with individual features peculiar to particular regions and particular periods. We can sometimes say whether a story or saying reflects Palestinian conditions, but we could not often by these means decide whether the conditions are those of Galilee in A.D. 29 or of Judaea in, say, A.D. 35–45. Yet we also need to examine the development of early Christianity against the background of the economic and social history of Palestine. That may enable us to understand and interpret some of the phases in the development of the movement.

ASPECTS OF THE ECONOMIC AND SOCIAL HISTORY

The ministry of Jesus took place in and around Galilee during the rule of the tetrarch Herod Antipas. The crucifixion of Jesus and the earliest phase of the Christian movement occurred in Judaea while Pontius Pilate was the governor. The Roman Emperor at the time was Tiberius, and he, like his predecessor Augustus, kept the budget under control. Heichelheim gives a favourable verdict on Claudius;[26] and Vespasian re-established political and economic order after the chaos he took over in A.D. 69. It was Nero who debased the coinage, and it was in the dark days of the mid sixties during Nero's reign that the economic problems of Palestine were most acute.

In Palestine the Romans probably exacted a tax of 12½ per cent of the harvest from the regions under their direct control. There was also a poll tax, and customs and transit duties. In Galilee under Antipas, the tetrarch himself took a substantial sum (200 talents from Galilee and Peraea, according to Jos. B. J. 2.95). Antipas may have had to pay tribute additionally to the Romans, but the matter is unclear.[27] What is clear is that pious Jews also paid a tithe, and a second tithe was either given to the poor or spent in Jerusalem. There were also first-fruits and other offerings to be made, and the institution of the Sabbath year meant that the land lay fallow once in seven years. The burden of civil and religious obligations was undoubtedly heavy. The precise amount is not easy to assess, but an estimate somewhere between 30 per cent and 40 per cent has been suggested.[28] It is small wonder that the rabbis needed rules about produce which had not been tithed, and that in regions paying tribute to Rome the taxes were resented. We know that Syria and Judaea protested about the taxes in A.D. 17.[29]

The Christian Church began in Jerusalem, the capital of the poor and doubly taxed land of Judaea. The city was an expensive one in which to live. Former Galilean fishermen had little chance of finding occasional employment there. Most of their converts were probably poor, and certainly included widows dependent on a daily distribution (Acts 6.1). Those among the converts to the new faith who had possessions, sold them and donated the proceeds to the apostles (Acts 4.34–7). The resident leaders and the poorer members of the new community were supported from such donations. The gifts were voluntary (Acts 5.4). This system differed from the community of goods practised at Qumran. There an isolated community lived a common life and co-operated to produce the necessities of life. Members of the sect were obliged to hand over their property on entry to the community, at least in the period when the Community Rule was first drawn up. The early Christians lived in Jerusalem, probably in different parts of the city, and had their own possessions, dwellings, and in many cases, presumably, employment. There was undoubtedly sale of property, and generosity, and a willingness to extend hospitality. But the similarity between the accounts of the Essenes and the accounts of the early Christians is due more to the literary descriptions of Philo, Josephus, and the author of Acts, than to close similarities between the actual movements.[30] This is not to deny that similarities exist, but to observe that the greatest similarities occur in the most literary parts of the relevant texts.

The persecution which initially affected the 'Hellenists' among the early Christians led to the spread of the community. No doubt the enforced departure of the Hellenists meant that further communities were established by those who, at least initially, arrived in need of hospitality and support. Certainly the emissaries of the

Jewish mission travelled without resources and in dependence on those who would accept them (Matt. 10.5–15, cf. Mark 6.8; Luke 9.3; 10.3–16). Paul states that he had waived the right to depend on his converts, though others in the Gentile mission exercised that right (1 Cor. 9.1–18, cf. 2 Cor. 11.7,20; 12.13). Certainly the new communities kept up the practice of supporting needy co-religionists, as help was sent to Jerusalem Christians during the famine of *c.* A.D. 48 (Acts 11.29) and later (2 Cor. 8—9). But this is to anticipate.

The pattern of the early years must have continued for some time but eventually external factors again became pressing. Under the Emperor Gaius the Jews threatened to leave their land unsown and to pay no tribute, rather than have their Temple defiled Jos. Ant. 18.274). But the threat did not materialize and in A.D. 41 Judaea again became a kingdom under Herod Agrippa I. Acts attributes the death of James the brother of John, to Herod Agrippa, and also the arrest of Peter (Acts 12.1–19). The new king spent extravagantly,[31] and engaged in great building projects, but was not extortionate (Jos. Ant. 19.299). The result of this policy was, presumably, immediate employment and subsequent debts. Agrippa was not averse to debts. His death in A.D. 44 meant that Judaea returned to direct Roman rule, taking Galilee with it. Our concern is not so much with events such as the troubles involving Theudas, but with the economic situation.

In the later forties famine struck Palestine. This was not a worldwide event, although there may have been shortages elsewhere. The evidence of Acts (11.28; 12.20) suggests that it took place during the reign of Claudius (A.D. 41–54), but not during Agrippa's reign (A.D. 41–4). This tallies with the details given by Josephus, who records it during the time of the governors Fadus and/or Tiberius Alexander (A.D. 44–8, cf. Jos. Ant. 20.101). It has been suggested that this famine was probably at its most severe during the year 47–8, as this was probably a Sabbath year when the fields lay fallow.[32] The effects of this must have been terrible, especially on the poorer citizens. Josephus and rabbinic sources record the generosity of the royal house of Adiabene to the people of Jerusalem, when many people were dying because they were unable to buy food.[33] Josephus also gives the price of an *'issārôn* of wheat (about four litres) during the famine as four drachmas (Jos. Ant. 3.320). The normal price was closer to one denarius for about thirteen litres of grain, and modern scholars have used this figure to calculate the effect of the famine. The figures suggest that the price of bread reached something like *thirteen times* the normal amount.[34]

If during the famine a whole day's wages bought less than a kilo of bread, it is no wonder that we hear of the urgent dispatch of money from Christians in Antioch to their brothers in Jerusalem (Acts 11.29), of solemn requests from Jerusalem Christians to Paul to 'remember the poor' (Gal. 2.10),[35] and bitter outcries in the gospels against the rich who feast while the poor starve (Luke 6.20–26; 16.19–31).

Though the famine was one of the worst hardships in this period, it is unlikely that the years which followed brought complete recovery. There was constant friction and we hear of allegations of corruption against some of the Roman governors. Felix, Albinus, and Florus were all hated. Acts 24.26 imputes venality to Felix.[36] Under him bands of robbers engaged in plunder and murder (Jos. Ant. 20.185–6) their ranks, no doubt, containing not only ardent nationalists but also those who had nothing to lose. We twice hear from Josephus of the high priestly party's seizing the dues of the priests, and that some of the poorer priests starved to death (Jos. Ant. 20.181, cf. 206).[37] Festus tried to bring order, but between his death and the arrival of Albinus (A.D. 62) the high priest Ananus had James the brother of Jesus, and others stoned to death (Jos. Ant. 20.200). Soon after this, Ananus was deposed. Albinus A.D. 62–4) is variously assessed. Josephus says he was guilty of extortion, and released prisoners for ransom money (B.J. 2.272–3). The sicarii used the technique of seizing hostages and bartering the freedom of their accomplices (Jos. Ant. 20.208–10). We also hear of rival bands warring against each other.[38] At about this time the building of the Temple ceased and thousands of workers became unemployed.[39] This may well have been, as Momigliano observed, a very significant factor in the troubles of the time. The authorities had to start plans for repaving the streets in order to reduce unemployment (Jos. Ant. 20.222).[40]

Josephus accuses Gessius Florus (A.D. 64–6) of massive extortion and of profiting from the plunder of the brigands (B.J. 2.278; Jos. Ant. 20.254–5). Florus seized seventeen talents from the Temple (B.J. 2.293), perhaps because the tribute was in arrears.[41] When the war began, the tribute certainly was in arrears (B.J.

2.404–5). Also significant is the fact that one of the first acts of the revolutionaries was, as often, to burn the debt registry (B.J. 2.426–7). It would be foolish to underestimate the religious and political causes of the war, but it is also clear that the economy of Judaea was in difficulties before the revolt. The defeat of the rebellion led to expropriations, and to a crisis in which, though corn was cheap, the lack of employment meant that people could not buy it.[42]

RETROSPECT AND PROSPECT

The foregoing outline of the economy, class structure, and economic and social history provides the backdrop against which our study must continue. The teaching in the gospels on poverty and wealth needs to be examined in the light of the factors we have sketched. The later evangelists Matthew and Luke were probably writing a decade or two after A.D. 70, and presumably in circumstances different from those of Palestinian Christians between A.D. 30 and A.D. 70. The sources probably come from communities of Christians nearer in time, and perhaps in locality, to the economic crises of A.D. 48–70. Earlier still are traditions which reflect the precarious economic circumstances of Christians in newly founded communities in and around Judaea. Prior to that again is the ministry of Jesus in Galilee and other parts of Palestine. If we examine these strata in sequence, starting with the latest and probing back to the oldest material, we may be able to test the hypothesis that there is some correlation between the economic circumstances we have sketched and the different strata of teaching on poverty and wealth in the gospels.

TWO

The Evangelists and their Sources

Our inquiry is concerned with the way that the gospels show Jesus and his disciples as leaving everything. This element of renunciation, and a distinct hostility to mammon and to earthly treasures, is widespread in the gospels. It is most marked in Luke, where the rich are most severely criticized (Luke 6.24–5; 12.20; 16.19–31), but we cannot simply attribute such severity to Luke. It is true that the Lucan beatitudes bless those who suffer poverty and hunger (Luke 6.20–21), while Matthew offers blessings on the poor 'in spirit'. Yet it is Luke who portrays Jesus as accepting financial support from women of wealth and influential position (Luke 8.3), or as the guest of a leading Pharisee (Luke 14.2). And even Matthew contains a parable about a merchant who sold everything he had in order to buy a pearl of great value (Matt. 13.46). We must acknowledge the diversity of the tradition and its redaction.

This means that we must examine the evidence of the gospels as a whole, and adopt a method of procedure which will bring the diversity and development of the tradition into focus. The method which will be adopted is to work back from the finished gospels, via their sources and traditions, towards the teaching of Jesus himself. We must ask how each evangelist understood the material he presents. We must ask how much material belongs to each of the sources, and how it seems to have been understood. We must then continue to ask questions about the oral tradition and the words of Jesus. The difficulties of such an enterprise are well known, and the fierce debates which have taken place over other aspects of the teaching of Jesus suggest that the results of this inquiry are likely to be tentative. There are, however, some criteria which may enable us to steer a course between the extremes of excessive scepticism and gross overconfidence in this area.

The first requirement in a study of the attitudes to wealth in the Synoptics is a comprehensive collection of the evidence. A complete list of passages cannot be included at this point, but some of the more striking passages have already been mentioned as examples of the material from the gospels to be discussed.[1] The evidence will be drawn chiefly from the Synoptics, as the Fourth Gospel contains little material of direct relevance to this particular topic, except perhaps for two passages which might imply the use of a common purse by Jesus and his disciples (John 12.6; 13.29).

MATTHEW'S REDACTION

The first step is to examine the redactional technique of Matthew and of Luke. This may give us some idea of the extent to which the evangelists modified the traditions and sources which they received. I propose to examine Matthew first and, in doing so, to pay particular attention to three aspects. These are his use of Mark, his use of the material presumably derived from Q, and the inclusion of any other material which seems to be derived from elsewhere. By adopting this procedure we can move from the more easily discovered to that which is less readily ascertainable.

When Matthew is compared with Mark, many of the passages about wealth and discipleship show only very minor variations. In Mark the first disciples leave their families and means of livelihood in order to follow Jesus. The picture in Matthew is the same. In the mission charge, Mark's account allows staff and sandals but forbids the taking of food and money for the journey. Matthew 10.10, however, forbids staff and sandals also. But Matthew is in this respect in agreement with Luke (9.3 and 10.4) against Mark 6.8. This would therefore seem to be due to his following another tradition, and not a sign of his greater severity than Mark. More significant may be the fact that whereas Mark forbids copper money and Luke silver, Matthew's version is different. His instructions to the twelve are: 'Do not *acquire gold* or silver or copper for your belts.' His mention of *gold* may be indicative of a legislator's desire to close all loopholes. On the other hand it is true that the money values mentioned in several places in Matthew are higher than those mentioned in the other gospels. Again it may be the case that his 'do not *acquire*' is less rigorous than the earlier 'do not *take*', but the difference is not great. Matthew, like Mark, expects disciples to be dependent on hospitality. But Matthew may well have belonged to a church which was wealthier than that for which Mark wrote.[2]

In two passages (15.19 and 13.22) Matthew lacks a disapproving reference to covetous desires which is found in the Marcan parallel. It may also be worth noting that at 19.18 Matthew lacks a reference to the tenth commandment (cf. Mark 10.19). Matthew, both here and in the Sermon on the Mount, shows an interest in the commandments, but says less than one might expect about the commandment which forbids covetousness. Certainly the many differences between the account of the rich man's refusal in Matthew 19 and in Mark 10 have long excited interest. Our present concern is with what is said about possessions. In this connection a number of small variants in Matthew's version may suggest that this evangelist felt a certain unease about the story he inherited from Mark. The variations are slight but they deserve careful attention.

In Mark the rich man is told: 'Go and sell what you have.' In Matthew 19.21 he is told: 'If you would be *perfect*, (*teleios*) go and sell your *possessions* (*ta hyparchonta*).' Some interpreters have argued that Matthew here introduces the idea of a double standard which distinguishes between those Christians who aim at perfection and those who do not. But it has frequently been observed that Matthew 5.48 stands in the way of such an interpretation in that it demands perfection of all, not just of some.[3] It therefore seems improbable that Matthew is advocating a fully articulated double standard. On the other hand it does seem to be the case that Matthew has modified the Marcan story. He has the rich man as told to sell 'possessions' rather than 'everything',[4] and he adds that it is hard for a *rich* man to enter the Kingdom, rather than hard for 'those who have money'. Moreover Matthew, who is not averse to recording harsh sayings against the Pharisees, seems to have omitted the charge that they 'devour the houses of widows' (Mark 12.40). He also lacks the story of the widow's mite (Mark 10.41–4). It could be argued that all these changes either improve the style, or are made in the interests of brevity. But it may be significant that such changes seem to occur regularly in passages critical of wealth. Matthew does seem less critical of riches than Mark.

It is obviously harder to examine Matthew's redaction of Q. When he and Luke differ, it is not easy to decide which might be further from the presumed source. Our attention must initially be directed to the first of the beatitudes. The difference between the two versions is immediately apparent. Luke beatifies the poor,

Matthew the poor *in spirit* (*ptōchoi tōi pneumati*). The literature on this subject grows year by year with unfailing regularity.[5] It is, however, our present concern simply to ask whether or not Matthew has toned down the presumed original. In discussing this one needs to bear in mind the complexities of *ʿānî* and *ʿānāw* in Hebrew, and the appearance of the phrase *ʿānᵉwê rûaḥ* in the Scrolls at 1Q Mil. 14.7.[6] The Semitic character of Matthew's version is not in doubt. It would, however, be a *non sequitur* to conclude from the Semitic flavour of Matthew's version that it must represent the original. We must consider not only the editing of the first beatitude, but also that of the entire set. Luke has four beatitudes followed by four woes (Luke 6.20–26). These bless those who are poor, hungry, weeping, and insulted. They utter woes for those who are rich, well fed, happy, and of good repute. The context makes it doubly clear that in Luke the poor are literally poor. They are also hungry, and they are contrasted with the rich and the well fed. Even without the woes, the Lucan beatitudes taken as a group refer to those who are literally poor and hungry. It will be argued later that this interpretation seems to be older than the Lucan redaction, or rather that Luke himself does not seem to have intensified the hostility to the rich which he found in his sources.[7]

In Matthew's beatitudes we find a different emphasis. The woes are absent, and there are eight (or nine) beatitudes. Most of these are concerned with moral qualities rather than with social disadvantage. This is clear from the inclusion of the meek, the merciful, the pure in heart, and the peacemakers. The poor are now poor *in spirit*,[8] and the hungry those who hunger and thirst *for righteousness*. The divergence between the two traditions is striking, and the emphasis in Matthew is clearly on religious and moral attitudes, rather than on the religious evaluation of actual destitution. The interpretation of Matthew seems clear enough. What is uncertain is whether or not he has amended the tradition he received. It is unlikely, as we shall see, that Luke has altered his tradition substantially, though it is possible that the two versions began to diverge before the final redaction. There is at least prima facie evidence for arguing that Matthew (or his predecessors) have modified the beatitudes by adding interpretative amplification. Taken in conjunction with the evidence derived from Matthew's editing of Mark we would then agree with those who conclude that Matthew exhibits less concern for 'the problems of actual want'.[9] (This does not wholly exclude the conjecture that Matthew was reinforcing an interpretation of the beatitudes which had always been possible.)

The tentative conclusion we have reached would be strengthened if we followed some texts of Matthew and omitted the reference to the poor in Matthew 11.5, but the longer text may be original. In some other passages, such as Matthew 6.19 and 23.26 it could be argued that Matthew is nearer to the original than the Lucan parallel. In both cases the Lucan version has an explicit emphasis on almsgiving which is absent or less sharp in the parallels in Matthew. At Matthew 6.33 (seek *first* his kingdom and his *righteousness* and *all* these things will be added to you) there may well be another example of Matthean interpretation by expansion. Far more significant is the fact that apart from the editing of sayings in Mark and Q there are very few fresh sayings added in Matthew which are critical of wealth.

There is always a danger of excessive subtlety in redaction studies. An examination of Matthew's treatment of sayings about wealth shows that such changes as there are, usually seem to be slight. On the other hand the tendency of the redaction seems clear. Matthew does not intensify the severity of sayings about riches, he makes such sayings somewhat less severe. This tendency may be correlated with the fact that the economic circumstances of Matthew's church seem to have been less harsh than those of the earlier Christian communities.

LUKE'S REDACTION

There has been frequent comment on the large amount of material in the Third Gospel on the subject of poverty and wealth.[10] Some commentators have attributed Ebionite tendencies either to Luke or to his source. Others have denied one, or the other, or even both of these propositions.[11] Careful appraisal is needed, and it is necessary both to note the many passages which are critical of riches, and to examine the editing of the tradition.

The first task is to make an overall survey of the relevant material in Luke, and to ask how much of it derives from the sources at the disposal of the author. Luke records the call of Levi, the mission charge, and the rich man's refusal, but these and other passages are presumably an inheritance from Mark. Similarly Luke records blessings on the poor (6.20), the call of disciples to leave home and family (9.57ff.), another version of the mission charge (10.4), an injunction against cares (12.22ff.), advice to lay up treasure in heaven (12.33), and a sharp antithesis between God and mammon (16.13). But all these have parallels or near equivalents in Matthew and are hardly to be attributed *in toto* to the inventiveness of Luke. It is true of course that some of the most severe statements about property and riches appear in Luke alone of the evangelists. It is in this gospel that we find woes uttered against the rich (6.24) and the cautionary tale of the rich fool (12.16–21) and of Dives and Lazarus (16.19–31). These and other passages appear only in Luke. But we need to ask whether it is more likely that Luke has invented, adapted, or inherited this additional material. But before putting that question it will be instructive to see how Luke has treated the material presumably derived from Mark and Q. If he has increased the severity of his source material where we can check what he has done, it is likely that he will have done the same where we are unable to check so easily. If he has not made such drastic alterations or additions to Mark and Q, then we may be more likely to conclude that his editorial treatment in other areas has been equally modest. We also need to bear in mind the relevance of Acts as evidence for the tendencies and propensities of the author of the two-volume work.

Once again the starting point is the editorial treatment of Mark. The first point to note is that the great majority of Marcan passages about wealth and property are retained by Luke.[12] Even when Luke lacks a direct parallel to the call of the disciples in Mark 1.16–20 we find that he has more than one equivalent passage elsewhere (cf. Luke 5.11 and 9.57–62). Luke avoids undue repetition but he does not avoid passages which portray discipleship in terms of renunciation. In some places he even adds sub-editorial touches which slightly increase the impact of such stories and sayings. This may well be only a sign of his fondness for the word 'all'. The disciples in Luke 'leave *all*' (5.11,28). The rich man is told to sell *all* that he has (18.21). Yet, curiously, a few verses later where Mark says 'we have left everything', Luke supplies 'we have left our property'.[13] Again, Mark mentions the leaving of house and family and lands, but Luke does not mention the lands (18.29). In the mission charge Luke does not, like Mark, allow staff and sandals, but this is probably due to the availability of another account in Q which seems to have influenced both Lucan versions.[14] There are other slight differences between Luke and Mark. Viewing this evidence as a whole, we could hardly say that Luke displays any consistent tendency to increase the severity of Mark's sayings about wealth.

The passages presumably derived from Q are less straightforward. The Lucan beatitudes certainly bless those suffering actual hunger, misery, persecution, and poverty (6.20–22). But the main differences from Matthew are, as we have seen, probably due to moralizing expansion by the latter, not to abbreviation by Luke. In that case the blessings on those in poverty are probably older than Luke's Gospel and derived from Luke's source. It is true that Luke also has woes against the rich and well fed. But we should probably attribute these also to a source, rather than to the inventiveness of the evangelist. There are similarities of wording between the Lucan woes and the Matthean beatitudes. It is unlikely that we should explain these similarities as due to the dependence of Luke on Matthew or vice versa. They could perhaps be due to both versions having the Greek of Isaiah 61 in mind. On the other hand it is most likely that the woes stood in the pre-Lucan tradition and that this accounts for the similarities in wording between them and the Matthean beatitudes. We must leave until later the question of the ultimate source of the beatitudes and the woes. For the moment we may simply conclude that it does not seem to have been Luke himself who originated the sentiments in 6.20–26. He is handing on tradition.[15] Luke was presumably in agreement with what he inherited from his sources here, and he may well have thought it relevant and applicable to his readers. But we need not attribute to him an *intensification* of hostility to wealth in these verses.

There are further passages where Luke also runs parallel to Matthew. In the mission charge Luke agrees with Matthew in being more severe than Mark. This again is presumably due to source material rather than to a tendency of the evangelist. In Luke 11.41 there is a curious phrase about almsgiving which seems to be based on a mistranslation of Aramaic, or a reinterpretation of it. The vocabulary of Luke 11.41, 'give for alms those things which are within ...' [RSV] is not strikingly redactional.[16] We must allow for a variation in Q, or else suspect that Matthew's 'cleanse the inside' is a 'correction' of what stood in Q. In Luke 12.33 we find 'sell your possessions, and give alms', while Matthew (6.19) has 'do not lay up for yourselves treasures on earth'. The selling of possessions and giving of alms is a frequent theme in Luke, and reappears in Acts, but the theme was already current in Luke's sources also. It is possible that Matthew has preserved the original and that Luke's tradition diverged, but it is also possible that Matthew 'improved' the saying.[17]

In other passages drawn from Q there is little indication that Luke has intensified the hostility to riches and to mammon. At Luke 6.30 the emphasis on giving to '*every one* who asks' is probably another example of the editorial touch noticed previously. In editing Mark and Q, Luke seems to have preserved much, and altered little, in the passages with which we are concerned. In Marcan contexts we even found an occasional softening. In Q contexts we may be correct to allow for the likelihood that an emphasis on almsgiving, and the woes against the rich, are to be attributed to source material rather than to the evangelist.

We are now in a position to consider the redaction of the special Lucan material. The woes perhaps belong here. Certainly we include here the story of Zacchaeus (19.1–10), the parable of the rich fool (12.16–21), and the tale of Dives and Lazarus (16.19–31). Attention should also be paid to the command to part with all possessions (14.33) and to the revocation of the mission charge (22.35–6). This list only includes the more striking items. For the most part the material consists of additional pericopae. There is every reason to suppose that these have been derived from a source or sources and edited in a similar way to the material derived from Mark and Q. If that view is correct then the main passages in Luke which are critical of wealth belong to a period prior to the evangelist. The latter includes them, occasionally adapts them, but also includes other material less critical of possessions. In the case of the special Lucan material we have the least evidence to go on for making decisions about the redaction. The best policy is inference from the redaction of the other sources. Arguments based on vocabulary can be rather precarious in view of the difficulty in establishing criteria in this area.[18]

What are we to make of the Lucan evidence as a whole? Compared with Matthew and Mark, Luke does appear more severe. But this impression is largely due to the inclusion of more material by Luke. We must also allow for Matthew's tendency to soften some of the harder sayings. The apparent severity in Luke is therefore largely to be attributed to his sources, and to the tradition which they contain.[19] A careful appraisal is needed. It is, of course, significant that Luke chooses to retain hard sayings about riches and the rich.[20] But we also need to note his literary skill, his knowledge of the world, and his obvious affinities with the relatively prosperous classes.[21] Luke's style places him among those with some knowledge of, and feeling for, literature. He is acquainted with the ways of commerce. Money, for him, is silver rather than copper. The financial illustrations in his Gospel are those of the medium-scale businessman.[22] Further, in Acts, and even in the Third Gospel, there is an interest in people of power and influence, towards whom the author seems not unsympathetic. While Luke retains many older sayings critical of riches, he may well do so, not because he himself is opposed to the rich, as some of his predecessors were, but because he wishes to give advice to the rich on how to use their wealth generously, and because he wishes to warn them of the danger of riches. The author is writing a two-volume literary apology to expound and commend Christianity as both true and politically innocent. He is writing for a wider public than the hearers of some of the sayings provided by his sources.[23] The economic circumstances of the evangelist and his readers do seem to have been easier and more comfortable than those endured by Christians of the preceding period. This difference is reflected in the way in which the evangelist has modified what he found in his sources. This difference is not as great as that between Matthew and his predecessors, but it does exist and traces of its effects can be noted.

THE SOURCES

We have now examined the editing by Matthew and Luke of passages about wealth, and are able to proceed to the next stage of the investigation. This is to press back behind the written gospels to the sources which they employed and to look at the tradition contained in those sources. I propose to include a brief study of Mark at this point, as the study of Mark has more affinities with the study of the sources than with that of those evangelists who used Mark. It will of course be appropriate, where possible, to look for signs of redactional activity in Mark and the sources Q and M and L. It will also be of considerable interest to compare the character of the material contained in the different sources.

Material peculiar to Matthew

The most striking fact about the special Matthean material is that it contains so few sayings about wealth. The relevant material from this source consists of the parables of the treasure and the pearl (Matt. 13.44–6, cf. Thomas log. 76,109); a saying about almsgiving (Matt. 6.3–4); a story about the Temple tax (17.24–7); and perhaps the parable of the sheep and the goats (25.31–46). This is a very small collection. It could be evaluated in various ways. The most one could make of it would be along the following lines.

The parables of the treasure and the pearl emphasize the surrender of 'whatever one has' (13.44,46). (This feature is missing or given less emphasis in the parallels in Thomas.) The parable of the sheep and the goats depicts Christians as hungry and thirsty wandering from place to place, and suffering nakedness, illness, and imprisonment.[24] One might also argue that the story of the Temple tax portrays Jesus as one who possessed no coin. The interpretation just suggested for these passages extracts the maximum of severity from the special Matthean material. But a more cautious estimate would suggest that M does not contain so much severity against wealth. First, the saying about almsgiving perhaps presupposes a normal capacity for giving. Secondly, the story about the Temple tax may simply contain reminiscence that Jesus and his disciples were impecunious wanderers. (The story hardly goes so far as to commend poverty.) Again, the parables of the treasure and the pearl do not necessarily place great emphasis on renunciation of property.[25] Nor is the interpretation of the parable of the sheep and the goats completely certain, though it undoubtedly has much to commend it.

It seems best to conclude that this stream of tradition contains only a few traces of real severity towards wealth. Even the endurance of hardship is only briefly mentioned. That there are a few traces is probably due to a stage in the tradition considerably earlier than the final Matthean redaction. The pre-Matthean tradition does contain some hard sayings on other topics too. The special Matthean material contains a few more hints of hostility to wealth than the tradition underlying the Fourth Gospel. But a comparison with the other sources will show that greater severity is found in them.

The Marcan Tradition

Our next task is to examine the relevant sections of the Gospel of Mark. We find here a group of passages which is by no means insignificant. Certainly Mark contains far more teaching of this character than does the Fourth Gospel. Also it includes a greater variety of such teaching than the special tradition in Matthew. But the Marcan material is not all of a piece, and we need to note which passages are generally thought to be editorial and which to belong to older tradition. This question is not a simple one. It is often held that the emphasis on suffering in the Gospel of Mark is a sign of something more than simple historical interest in the fate of Jesus.[26] Our concern is, however, not so much with suffering as with passages in which renunciation is encouraged or required. These, it would seem, are traditions inherited by the evangelist. The reason for thinking this is that there do seem to be occasional phrases which modify an earlier rigorism. One example of this may be in the limited concessions made in the Marcan version of the mission charge (Mark 6.8ff.). This is, as we have noted above, slightly less severe than the version in Matthew and Luke presumably influenced by Q. We might also detect a reaction from a more severe outlook in some of the sayings in Mark 10. In 10.24a and 26–7 the disciples express amazement at the hard saying about the camel and the eye of the needle.[27] Such surprise could serve the dramatic purpose of intensifying the effect of the saying in question. On the other hand the comforting theological assertion that 'with God all things are possible' is probably intended as a reassurance rather than an intensification of the demand. Moreover, verses 24, 26, and 27 are more concerned with the general difficulty of entry into the Kingdom, whereas verses 23 and 25 speak about the problem for the rich.

It may be then that the final editing of Mark included phrases which drew back from the severity towards possessions which characterized the earlier tradition. But we certainly find many passages in the Marcan tradition which express that severity. The interpreter of the parable of the sower spoke of the 'seduction of wealth' (4.19), and the compiler of the list of vices in Mark 7 included covetousness in his catalogue (7.22). We also find in the tradition a warning about gaining the whole world and losing one's soul (8.36). This teaching in its Marcan context probably reflects the sentiment of early Christianity. Those who handed on the tradition were aware that membership of the Church offered few financial attractions, and that men refused to become Christians or ceased to be such for worldly reasons. That experience may be reflected in the sayings just discussed.[28]

In addition to this there is also the teaching on discipleship. This is prominent in Mark, but its prominence is probably due to his sources. It may well be the case that Mark drew his material from older collections of sayings and stories. Most significant among these stories for our purposes are the accounts of the call of the first disciples (Mark 1.16–20, cf. 2.14), and the call of the rich man (Mark 10.17ff.). In the case of the first, it is the break with the past and the decision to 'follow' Jesus which is emphasized more than the renunciation of property and means of livelihood. In the case of the invitation to the rich man, the question of wealth comes right into the foreground. Presumably in early Christian times the story was used as an exemplary tale for prospective disciples. To become a Christian involved more than keeping the law of Moses. A convert was expected to 'follow' Jesus and to distribute his goods to 'the poor'. Such a use for the story in the tradition would be in keeping with the picture of the Church given in Acts. It is also in keeping with the situation depicted there that the tradition included sayings on the extreme difficulty of the rich gaining entry to the Kingdom (Mark 10.23b,25), and on the compensations of the common life in the Church for those who had made the necessary sacrifice (Mark 10.28–30).

The teaching which Mark presumably derived from his sources matches well with some of the features of early Christian life which may be gleaned from Acts. There were disciples like Barnabas, who sold property and handed over the proceeds to assist the poor within the community. Such men were commended. So the Marcan tradition encouraged converts to break with their old life and to follow the example of the first disciples. If they had possessions, like the rich man, they were encouraged to sell them and give the proceeds to the poor. This picture tallies with the rules for early Christian missionaries who were urged to take no money with them on their journeys. The earliest Church found that few rich men entered its ranks. At a later stage in the formation of Mark's Gospel we may be right to detect signs of a slight modification of the earlier outlook, and some anxiety about its severity. This process of routinization seems to have gone further in Matthew, however, than in Mark, to judge from our earlier discussion. That would correspond with the few indications we have about the composition of the two communities. Mark's rough and simple style, his assumption that money is 'copper' (6.8) and his seeming preference for villages and the country rather than cities[29] contrast with the greater wealth of Matthew's church[30] and the greater sophistication of Luke's readers. Besides, the expectation of suffering and persecution is very much alive in Mark's Gospel.

The Q Material

We must next consider the material common to Matthew and Luke but absent from Mark, or differently reported by Mark. If we are able to find sayings and stories here which differ from Mark in detail, but agree with the Marcan material in their general import, then this will be of considerable interest. One of the criteria used in analysis of the gospels is that of multiple attestation. If a theme or sentiment is found independently in more than one of the sources, or in more than one of the oral forms, this strengthens its claim to belong to the earlier strata of the tradition closest to the teaching of Jesus.

The theological outlook of the community or communities which produced Q has also been a matter of considerable debate in recent scholarship. There have been several studies of the theology and redaction of Q, and at least one full-scale, if somewhat idiosyncratic, commentary.[31] Q's interest in the Son of Man need not detain us here, but the eschatological character of the document clearly has a bearing on what it says about wealth and property. Q contains prophetic and wisdom sayings designed to guide a community which saw itself as living in the last days. That community was also aware of itself as suffering from opposition and persecution. All these factors would tend to encourage such a community to hold mutual aid in high regard, and to despise the worldly advantages possessed by its opponents, but which held little attraction for those expecting the appearance of Jesus as Son of Man in the immediate future.

Q displays a more distinct interest in the subject of possessions than any of the sources we have so far considered. Here we find that the poor are promised the Kingdom (Luke 6.20, cf. Matt. 5.3). It is they who are the recipients of the good news (Luke 7.22; Matt. 11.5). It is very likely that the early Church in Jerusalem described itself as poor; it certainly was impoverished in the period of Paul's missionary activity, when aid was supplied from Christians in Antioch and elsewhere. The term 'poor' could indeed include the idea of dependence on God, but the religious associations by no means exclude the reference to real need. In adopting this self-description the early Christians were continuing a tradition which ran through Judaism from the psalms to the pseudepigrapha, and is also found in the Qumran texts.[32] The faithful poor endure oppression and hardship and look to God for recompense. The expectation of recompense and of future reversal of fortune, as well as a conviction that innocent hardship and suffering is an indication of righteousness, these are often found in religious groups suffering economic disprivilege and social rejection.[33] This element is less prominent in Matthew's version of the beatitudes than in Luke's rendering, but we have already noted the tendency of Matthew to adapt the interpretation of his sources to his own rather different circumstances.

Q, like Mark, contains passages concerned with discipleship and mission. These emphasize that one who 'follows' Jesus must expect to sever his ties with home and family (Luke 9.57ff.; Matt. 8.19–22). The similarity with Mark indicates that this motif is older than either Mark or Q, and these sayings may have applied originally to those who accompanied Jesus during his ministry. In their present setting, however, they certainly reflect the sacrifices demanded of those exercising an itinerant ministry, perhaps of disciples generally. In Luke's version these brief narratives immediately precede the sending of the seventy. If that had been the case also in Q[34] then the context would suggest that it is primarily wandering missionaries who are expected to sever all previous ties.

We have already noted that the mission charge in Q forbids staff and sandals as well as a bag and either purse or money. Q seems to have lacked the two concessions which we find in Mark.[35]

The Q material suggests that early Christianity in Syria–Palestine adopted and applied to itself the promises to the poor, and turned the itinerant ministry of Jesus and his disciples into grounds for legislation about the equipment of missionaries. It also adopted sayings critical of earthly wealth. It shared with Judaism a distaste for 'mammon' and pressed the need to choose between God and possessions.[36] So also it shared with Judaism what was probably a common sentiment at the time of the famine of *c.* A.D. 48, urging the acquisition of heavenly treasures.[37] Certainly it seems to have been during that period of widespread hardship that the charitable dispersal of earthly treasure was interpreted as storing up treasure of a more permanent kind in heaven. We find this motif both in Q and in the rabbinic tradition. The latter specifically attributes the sentiment to the period of the famine. No doubt the Q community would have found similar relevance in its version of the saying during that particular period of acute distress.

Both in Matthew and in Luke the saying on treasures is linked with the diatribe against care. The order differs in the two gospels, but both passages may have been part of a short catechism in Q on the subject of discipleship.[38] The material has, however, passed through many stages. We do not possess precise criteria for assigning each section to a particular point. Occasionally we can detect the editorial work of the evangelists. To discover editorial elements in Q is much more difficult. We can, however, ask about the life setting of individual oral units and we can look at the character of the total collection in Q. We can also compare Q with the other sources. Even to do this involves surmise and conjecture. It would, however, be eminently reasonable to see in Q the teaching of a community which was much poorer than the church or churches for which Matthew was writing. Mark may have been read by poor Christians in some Graeco-Roman city, but the material in his Gospel also reflects the difficulties of rural Palestine. That latter feature is even more marked in Q which must to some extent reflect the difficulties of Christian communities in the period between the famine of *c.* A.D. 48 and the Jewish revolt some two decades later.

Q then contains prophetic utterances of blessing on the poor.

It contains stories and rules which urge disciples and missionaries to dispense with all but the minimum necessities of life. It contains exhortations to store treasure in heaven by exercising generosity, and to overcome care and the service of mammon. With this collection we may compare the material in the other sources. Clearly Q contains far more than M, but when compared with Mark a fair degree of similarity emerges. Mark also contains a mission charge and stories about the call of disciples which commend the abandonment of ties and possessions. The story of the rich man in Mark 10 also speaks of treasure in heaven as the reward for giving away possessions here and now. The impossibility of serving God and mammon is hinted at in other terms in the saying about the camel and the needle's eye. Mark lacks the prophetic blessings on the poor found in Q and also has no equivalent for the poetic denunciation of cares.

When we turn to the material recorded only in Luke, however, a different comparison results. Here we find an outlook even fiercer and harsher than the already striking passages in Mark and Q.

Material found only in Luke

The precise origin and nature of Luke's special source or sources is one of the many enigmas of New Testament study. The infancy narratives are certainly different in style and content from the rest of Luke's special material. Much of the rest is found in Q contexts, though by no means exclusively so. The theory has often been propounded that all the non-Marcan material originally formed a 'proto-Luke', complete with infancy narratives and passion narrative as well as the sayings material of Q and L. In its full form this theory has not met with general acceptance. The existence of a separate pre-Lucan passion narrative is open to doubt, and the cohesion of proto-Luke without the Marcan elements is debatable. While the full proto-Luke theory remains an interesting speculation, one cannot dismiss so readily the possibility of an enlarged *sayings* source consisting of Q and L. Luke tends to keep his sources separate, and to follow first Mark and then Q. Yet the L sayings material is often found in Q contexts. Attempts to distinguish L from Q on linguistic grounds are fraught with difficulty[39] and so we cannot exclude the possibility of a closer link between Q and L. It could be that some of the material found only in Luke was in Q, and was omitted by Matthew.[40] It could also be the case that Luke's version of Q had been expanded with additional material. All these considerations mean that we should not hastily assume that all the special Lucan material, conveniently but loosely designated L, formed one coherent source. We do, however, need to look at this collection of possibly disparate material which is to be found in Luke's Gospel alone. Our procedure will be briefly to examine each passage in turn in Luke's order.

In the infancy narratives the Magnificat contains the *locus classicus* for an expression of hostility to the rich: 'the rich he has sent empty away' (Luke 1.53). It is significant that the rich who are sent away empty are contrasted with the hungry who are filled with good things. Poverty meant actual want, especially hunger, while riches meant a full table. The phrases echo the wording of the psalms (especially Psalm 106.9, LXX). The tenses, though past, celebrate the beginning of the fulfilment of hopes about the future, and the whole context seems to belong to a Jewish or Jewish Christian psalm expecting reversal of fortune in the new age.[41] It derives from a long tradition of Jewish eschatology expecting the fate of the pious sufferers to be reversed when God vindicates his people. In different contexts this is the expectation of Israel, or of groups within Israel, or subsequently of suffering Jewish Christians.[42] The psalm could be the product of Jewish Christianity, or adapted from Judaism or from disciples of John the Baptist. What is especially interesting from our point of view is the similarity between this and other special Lucan material. We shall find reversal of fortune expected also in the woes and in the parable of Dives and Lazarus.

At Luke 3.10–14 we find additional teaching attributed to John the Baptist on the subject of sharing clothing and food with those in need. This and the advice against greed (here given to tax collectors and soldiers) is all in line with the normal moral teaching of the period and especially with Jewish teaching on almsgiving. Luke presumably derived it from one of his sources.[43] At Luke 4.18 we encounter Luke's longer version of the sermon at Nazareth. With echoes of Isaiah 61.1 and of 58.6, this corresponds to some extent to the blessings on the poor which we also find in the beatitudes. There are also affinities with the reply to John. Some regard the passage as a Lucan adaptation of Mark, but Schürmann provides a carefully argued case for regarding it as a Lucan editing of a passage from one of his other sources, probably Q.[44]

The woes on the rich and the well fed at Luke 6.24–6 are clearly of prime importance for our theme. Here we have an explicit prophetic utterance of doom upon the rich. The woes match the four Lucan beatitudes point by point. Some have attributed them to the evangelist himself, but we have already shown reason to doubt that it was Luke who was bitter towards the rich. Further considerations are the similarities of wording between the woes and the Matthean beatitudes, and the similar woes to be found in James, as well as the non-Lucan vocabulary.[45] The woes would seem to be pre-Lucan. They presumably reflect a period of hardship when the pious poor were starving while the rich feasted. If the woes are a Christian composition then they could derive from any hard-pressed group during the difficult early decades of the Christian movement, but perhaps the period of the famine of *c.* A.D. 47–8 was a time when tensions of this kind must have been especially acute. As with the Magnificat and also with the parable of Dives and Lazarus, the theology expressed is one which hopes for future reversal of fortune to compensate the sufferings and injustices of the present. Like those other passages the woes are in continuity with works such as the Admonitions of Enoch and the Qumran Psalms in this respect.[46]

Some have attributed the composition of the woes to Luke, but it seems more likely that they are pre-Lucan. Some attribute them to L, others to Q. In favour of the latter view is the obvious connection with the beatitudes, the fact that Q material also follows the woes in Luke, that Matthew does tend to tone down passages hostile to wealth, and above all that traces of the vocabulary of the woes appear in the Matthean beatitudes.[47]

At Luke 6.34–5 we meet the exhortation to lend without expecting repayment. This is simply part of the general teaching on generosity widespread in the sources, and no doubt especially relevant in the straitened circumstances of the early Christians. The context is that of Q and the parallel with 6.30 suggests that 6.34–5 belongs to the larger whole or is a pre-Lucan addition to it.

Luke 8.3 mentions, whether out of historical reminiscence or as models of generosity, the women who supported Jesus and the twelve. This is an approximate equivalent of Mark 15.41 in a more appropriate position in the narrative. As it contains additional detail it may not all have been derived from Mark, though Luke does sometimes move Marcan material to aid the sequence of his narrative.

More important is a series of passages in Luke 12 on the subject of riches and possessions. These clearly appear in a Q context, whether from Q or not.[48] Luke 12.13–15 portrays Jesus as refusing the role of mediator in a dispute over property and as uttering warnings against greed. The sentiments are not out of keeping with what can be ascertained of Jesus's character. But it is the sequel which is more striking. The parable of the rich fool mocks a man who stores a rich harvest which he does not live to enjoy. It is the concluding verse (12.21) which indicates the way in which the parable was interpreted by the tradition. The storing of earthly treasures is vulnerable to the vicissitudes of life, and to destruction and death; generosity (being rich towards God) brings no such disappointment. The message is similar to that of the saying on treasures, which indeed follows a little later at Luke 12.33. In fact this message is more explicit in Luke 12.33 where the Lucan parallel to 'Do not lay up for yourselves treasures on earth' (Matt. 6.19) runs 'Sell your possessions, and give alms'. The source and redaction critics are in evident disarray over the variation here between Matthew and Luke,[49] but the commendation of generosity and the denunciation of hoarding are implied or demanded in both versions and presumably derive from Q.

In Luke 14 we find variations preceding, and in the course of, the parable of the great supper. The Lucan version of the parable specifically mentions the invitation to the poor, the maimed, the blind, and the lame (14.21). This point is anticipated at Luke 14.12. The exhortation to invite the poor rather than one's kin or 'rich neighbours' is probably a Lucan interpretation of the parable—the vocabulary of verse 12 seems to be Lucan[50]—but we cannot exclude the possibility of a variant interpretation of the parable in whichever source Luke was following here.

Luke 14.33 comes towards the end of a section on the demands of discipleship. The claims of discipleship outweigh those of family, demand the bearing of a cross (14.26–7) and the surrender of all possessions: 'So therefore, whoever of you does not renounce all that he has cannot be my disciple' (14.33). But this last demand is separated from the earlier ones by the parable of the man who builds a tower and the king who goes to war. It looks like an addition to the earlier demands.[51] It is, of course, quite in keeping with the story of the rich man in Mark 10, or with the stories of would-be disciples in Luke 9.57–62. This saying is, however, a statement applying not just to particular individuals but to anyone who wishes to be a disciple. If we are right in arguing above that Luke himself has not intensified the hostility to wealth which he found in his sources, then we should assign the formulation of this verse to pre-Lucan tradition. In that case it matches passages such as the parable of the rich fool and the injunction to sell earthly treasures which we noted in Luke 12, but goes rather further than either. But to which source should we assign it?

The parable of the unjust steward in Luke 16.1–8 is probably best understood as one of the eschatological parables of Jesus, in spite of ingenious attempts to interpret it otherwise.[52] The group of sayings which follow it, however, show how the parable was interpreted in the tradition. These supplementary sayings are linked by the catchword 'mammon'. One of them (Luke 16.13) is usually assigned to Q because its statement that it is impossible to serve two masters is almost identical with Matthew 6.24. Yet Luke 16.13 is clamped to 16.9 and 16.11 by the catchword 'mammon' which again shows how difficult it is to assign material to sources. The force of 16.9 is to urge the disposal of 'unrighteous mammon' with the promise that the beneficiaries of such charity will ensure the giver a home in eternity. The message is similar to that of many previous injunctions to charity, such as the saying about treasures. The expression 'unrighteous mammon' raises the question whether this means ill-gotten gain as some Jewish texts suggest, or whether all wealth is castigated here. Dupont argues that wealth is here seen as a trust from God abused when appropriated exclusively.[53] Certainly in 16.13 it is mammon as such which is opposed without further qualification. These verses stem from one or other of the sources. Those who composed them may not have regarded possessions as evil in themselves, but they certainly regarded the hoarding and accumulation of wealth as evil. They may also have suspected the rich of unjust acquisition. That was certainly the case at Qumran when the poor members of the sect denounce wealth, unjust gain, and the greed and oppression of the Wicked Priest.[54] But the passage in Luke is less severe than some of the Qumran texts. All the same, the hostility of 'the poor' to the rich and to 'unrighteous mammon' in Luke's sources should not be underestimated.

In Luke 16.14 there is an accusation of love of money directed against the Pharisees. Before assuming that such a charge was justified, one should first remember the very extensive commendations of almsgiving in rabbinic literature. The verse makes an awkward transition from condemnation of mammon to accusations of self-justification. Dupont points to Lucan features in the verse and regards it as probably redactional, but Schürmann thinks it probably part of Q.[55] The verse reflects hostility between church and synagogue and perhaps tells us more about the accusations which were made than about the behaviour of the Pharisees.[56] Luke may have recast the verse but it probably comes from earlier anti-pharisaic polemic, just as Luke 20.47 derives from Mark 12.40.

The parable of Dives and Lazarus must be given more detailed attention at a later point. Here we may anticipate some of the conclusions of that discussion, and concentrate on the parable as a feature of pre-Lucan source material. The parable probably makes use of a traditional tale, which also appears in Jewish sources. Though the rich man's unbelief and lack of concern for the poor are hinted at in the parable, these features are not directly emphasized as the reason for his condemnation. In fact the man's wealth seems to be the main reason for his translation to Hades, and this has given commentators considerable difficulty. But the portrayal of the rich man is not unique in the material found only in Luke. It matches the outlook of the woes (which we have had some reason to assign to Q) and that of the Magnificat (which belongs to the infancy narratives in Luke). In both these other places a reversal of fortune is proclaimed in which the rich are overthrown by God and the hungry are filled with good things. In the context of pre-Lucan Christianity it was no doubt assumed that the rich in question were those who failed to help the poor, did not believe the Christian proclamation of resurrection, and even (Luke 6.22–3) persecuted Christianity. Though Dupont is able to point to many Lucan touches in the parable, Degenhardt lists many non-Lucan features of vocabulary and style.[57] That it comes from a source we need not doubt, and it is usually assigned to L. Against that it might be possible to argue for a connection with the Q parable of the great feast (both use the story of Bar Ma'jan). One could also point to the affinity to the woes *if* those belong to Q.

A few features such as 'Hades', 'consolation', and already having received one's reward could be paralleled from Matthew. But these are hardly conclusive grounds on which to determine allocation to one source rather than another.

The story of Zacchaeus in Luke 19.2–10 describes the salvation of a repentant Judaean tax collector who promises to give half his goods to the poor, and repay fourfold anyone whom he has defrauded. As tax collectors were notorious for extortion, the story hardly assumes that Zacchaeus would be affluent after making amends. Some regard Luke 19.8 as breaking the sequence of 19.7 and 19.9 and as a later insertion.[58] If so, the addition could still be pre-Lucan.

One of the more puzzling passages must be Luke 22.35–6 which seems to revoke some of the rules of the mission charge. This urges disciples to take a purse and a bag with them and even to buy a sword. We are at present concerned with the question of sources rather than with whether such a volte-face is attributable to Jesus. One might see it as an attempt by Luke to soften the rigour of the rules of the mission charge, and at the same time to account for the use of a sword in Gethsemane. But the vocabulary suggests that the passage is pre-Lucan.[59] At some point the earlier rules (in Q) about travelling without purse, or bag, or weapon were reversed. Perhaps the most likely explanation is that during a time of upheaval, perhaps during the revolt, the earlier rules were reversed. It is hard to think that the rules of the mission charge were still observed at a time when this passage was also current. All the same the mention of the sword is both striking and not readily explicable.[60]

Retrospect

We are now in a position to evaluate the material recorded only in Luke. The difficulty of doing this is especially acute because of the number of factors for which allowance needs to be made. Idiosyncrasies could be due to redaction by Luke, to omission from or alteration of Q by Matthew, to pre-Lucan expansion of Q, or to the existence of a special source or sources. We have seen that redaction by Luke is the least likely explanation in the great majority of cases. Though in some passages there are traces of Lucan redaction, those who have closely examined the vocabulary have usually noted many non-Lucan features pointing to Luke's use of older material. The most likely candidates for evaluation as Lucan amendment are 14.12, 14.21, and 8.3, but not even these are certain. This confirms our earlier conclusion that Luke does not intensify the hostility to wealth which came from his sources. We based this view initially on a study of Luke's treatment of Mark, but it has stood up to further investigation.

Another of our earlier conclusions might also be extended. This was that Matthew tended to soften the hostility to wealth which he found in his sources. Another whole series of passages might represent omissions from Q by Matthew. These include Luke 3.10–14; 4.18; 6.24–6; 6.34–5; 12.13–21; and perhaps 16.14. There could also be alteration by Matthew which would account for Matthew 6.19 differing from Luke 12.33. It is important to emphasize that the arguments relating to these passages are far from conclusive. Of these passages some are simply condemnations of hoarding, covetousness, and extortion, while others commend almsgiving or lending without return. Matthew is not always completely without equivalent for some of these motifs, though he certainly lacks anything similar to the woes. It is the omission of the woes by Matthew which is the most interesting instance of this suspected tendency. Matthew does seem to have wording which matches some of the words used in the woes, and his expansion of the beatitudes may represent a compensation for the omission of the woes.

We cannot, however, account for all the hostility to the rich by assigning it to passages from Q omitted by Matthew. The best example to the contrary is Luke 1.53 which comes from the infancy narratives. The complete independence of Matthew and Luke in this area is one of the strongholds of the conventional source-critical hypotheses of modern times. One at least of Luke's special sources celebrated poetically God's overthrow of the rich and compensation to the hungry. But on stylistic ground the infancy narratives are distinct from the rest of the material found only in Luke. The parable of Dives and Lazarus represents the most lurid description of the fate of the heedless rich. This should presumably be assigned to the special Lucan source or sources along with the story of Zacchaeus and also the injunction in 14.33 that disciples should give up all possessions. But reliable grounds for distinguishing what is to be assigned to Q and what to L are not at present available for passages which lack parallels in Matthew. It could be that some of these passages are also from Q. It is also quite possible that the passages listed in the previous paragraph are to be assigned to L. We must recognize the uncertainty at this point. What is certain is that the greater severity evident in Luke's Gospel is not due to the evangelist but to his inclusion of material from either Q or L which is unknown to Mark and lacking in Matthew.

COMPARISON OF THE SOURCES

We can now proceed to the next stage of our investigation which is to compare the contents of the sources as far as is possible. We noted initially that there was an approximate gradation from M which contained little hostility to wealth through Mark and Q (which contained passages about discipleship and renunciation, and rules for wandering missionaries) to material only in Luke, where the most insistent teaching on almsgiving and the most lurid condemnations of the rich are to be found. Closer examination has shown reason to modify this picture to a certain extent. We must allow for the tendency of Matthew to tone down or omit harsh sayings about wealth. This means that the apparent mildness of M may be misleading. Certainly this source does not give as full a picture of early Christian criticism of wealth in the period prior to that of the evangelists. We should therefore take the more seriously such glimpses of both hardship and severity as do survive in M. On the other hand the apparent severity of L may be less extreme than appears at first sight. Certainly it is not to be attributed to Luke himself. Nor is it *all* necessarily to be attributed to L. The uncertainty which must continue over the demarcation between Q and L means that we must allow for the possibility that some at least of the hard sayings originally stood in Q.

Q certainly contained blessings on the poor which do not appear in Mark. Q also contained the categorical statement that one cannot serve God and mammon. Either Q, or L, or both, contained passages expecting a reversal of fortune in which the rich would suffer deprivation and torment (e.g. the woes, and the parable of Dives and Lazarus). In addition to this, the Lucan infancy narratives contain a somewhat similar, but less lurid, expectation that God will fill the hungry with good things and send the rich away empty. This reversal theology is a Christian equivalent of what is also found in the psalms and in sectarian and apocalyptic Jewish writings. Such a motif is also to be found in James and in Revelation as we note on page 44.[61] But how far do Q and/or L go beyond Mark in this respect? Mark 10 includes the story of how Jesus asked the rich man to give his property to the poor. The same chapter also includes the saying that it is harder for a rich man to enter the Kingdom than for a camel to go through the eye of a needle. This passage is indeed followed by one which offers those who surrender property now compensations both here and in the hereafter, when 'many that are first will be last, and the last first' (Mark 10.29–31). We can find hopes of apocalyptic reversal in Mark also. But in Mark more emphasis is placed on future compensation for those who make renunciations in the present. Mark does not give us lurid descriptions of the future fate of those who enjoy present prosperity. On the other hand Mark does agree with Q in portraying disciples of Jesus as people who were expected to abandon both family and possessions for the Kingdom. There is also general though not complete agreement between Mark and Q over the amount of impedimenta that itinerant Christian missionaries were permitted to take with them.

As for the sources, our conclusions can now be summarized. Though we have seen reason to qualify excessive differentiation of the sources, differences of emphasis and of outlook remain. In the traditions contained in the Fourth Gospel we find only occasional glimpses of early Christian attitudes to property. In the Synoptics the situation is different. Even M reveals traces of severity and evidence of the suffering of hardship. Q and L are more severe than the Marcan tradition in some respects, though Mark supports their evidence in others. A theology of retribution on the rich appears especially in passages found only in Luke, but this may not all be attributable to one source. Even this therefore is distributed across more than one source and is not the witness of a single line of tradition.

We have concluded that in general it is to the sources rather than to the evangelists that we should attribute the severity towards wealth which is found in the gospels. It is not possible to assign the documents to particular localities with any confidence, and even attempts to date them can only be approximations. We would, however, be correct to regard the sources as closer to Palestinian Christianity before the Jewish revolt. The evangelists Matthew and

Luke were probably writing elsewhere and after that period. The greater severity attributable to the sources correlates with the harsher economic circumstances of Christianity prior to the Jewish revolt. It was a time when, for example, Paul was attempting to raise money from poor converts in Greek cities to help even poorer co-religionists who were impoverished after the famine. The situation of Matthew and Luke was different, and their outlook less severe, especially that of Matthew. But we must now turn away from the evangelists and their sources to consider earlier phases of the gospel tradition.

THREE

Hostility to Wealth in the Oral Tradition

We must now ask how much of the teaching in the sources about property and riches actually derives from Jesus himself, and how much is due to the tradition. This question is far from easy to answer in view of the well-known difficulties of the quest for the historical Jesus. There are criteria which help us to decide what derives from Jesus and what is to be attributed to the tradition. But these criteria are far from complete or decisive in every instance. If we can build up some picture of the character of primitive Christianity during the period of the oral tradition, that will help us go some way in resolving this problem.[1]

HISTORICAL BACKGROUND

The period in question covers the years from *c.* A.D. 30 until *c.* A.D. 70. During that time Palestinian Christians underwent at least three major economic crises. The first was the difficult initial founding of the Christian community in Jerusalem. A second was the famine of *c.* A.D. 48. A third was the worsening crisis in the sixties when economic pressure, national feelings, and religious resentment built up to the Jewish revolt of A.D. 66. We might perhaps look briefly at each of these crises in turn.

The nucleus of the primitive Church in Jerusalem consisted of disciples who had followed Jesus from Galilee until his execution in Jerusalem. When Paul visited Jerusalem some years later, Peter and John were still among the 'pillars' of this community (Gal. 2.9). This evidence tallies with that of Acts that Peter, James, and John were the founders of the Jerusalem church (James the son of Zebedee later being replaced by James the brother of Jesus). Now this new community was not only politically suspect, as its leaders were disciples of someone executed for messianic pretensions; it was also economically precarious. Peter, James, and John were former Galilean fishermen. The only fishing they would do in Jerusalem would be carried on as 'fishers of men'. Acts 4. 32–5 records that the earliest converts to the new faith sold their property and laid the proceeds at the apostles' feet. This money was no doubt used in part to sustain poorer members of the new community, but it was also used to support the apostles as preachers of the new creed. Again this evidence from Acts is supported by that of Paul. Though Paul himself renounced the right of an apostle to earn his living from the gospel, he regards it as a principle commanded by the Lord himself (1 Cor. 9.1–14). The twin practices of supporting apostles, and of aiding poorer co-religionists, remained characteristic of the community. It was this practice which was in Acts (and elsewhere) described as fulfilling the ideals of Deuteronomy and of Greek utopianism.[2] The language about having 'all things in common' belongs to the literary world of Luke. But it corresponds to an historical reality in early Christianity, namely the high degree of mutual aid practised in the community.

We can now see how some of the sayings and stories of the gospel tradition fit this *Sitz im Leben*. We need not necessarily assume that these stories and sayings arose at this time. In some cases they may well be older, and originate in the teaching of Jesus. Whether they originated then, or in the early days of the Christian community, they would have acquired added significance in the circumstances which we have just described. We can see the aptness for this period of the rule that Christian missionaries should travel without impedimenta, and trust themselves to the customary hospitality of the Ancient Near East. We can also see how Christian converts were no doubt spurred to generous support of the cause by tales of the sacrifices and renunciation made by named and unnamed disciples. Clearly we must look in more detail at the rules and at the stories, with this factor in mind.

The second economic crisis for early Palestinian Christianity was the famine of A.D. 47–8. We can now see that the earlier sale of capital assets in order to support the community was not the policy of foolish idealism that some have imagined. No doubt the expectation of an imminent apocalypse encouraged a less than prudent attitude to such assets. But the need to support apostles and to aid poorer members of the community provided an immediate occasion for such a policy. What caused economic ruin to the community was neither their historical generosity, nor their legendary 'love-communism', but the disastrous famine. Possibly compounded by the incidence of the Sabbath year when fields lay fallow, the famine caused the price of bread to leap to thirteen times the normal level.[3]

Starvation and death ensued. Josephus and rabbinic sources record the generosity of the royal house of Adiabene to the citizens of Jerusalem at this time;[4] and we hear also of the urgent dispatch of money from Christians in Antioch to their brothers in Jerusalem, and of solemn requests from Jerusalem Christians to Paul to 'remember the poor' (Acts 11.29; Gal. 2.10).

If we are to look for a *Sitz im Leben* for passages which denounce the rich who feast while others starve, we need look no further. What was always a problem in the sharply stratified society of Palestine was now a matter of life and death. We can understand, therefore, the fierceness with which the woes on the rich and the well fed would have been uttered in this situation. The story of Dives and Lazarus, and the tale of the rich fool, would also have seemed especially apposite at this time. So too would exhortations to generosity and denunciations of hoarding have seemed timely and appropriate.

The third great crisis for Palestinian Christianity was the ill-fated Jewish revolt of A.D. 66–70. Itself in part the product of worsening economic oppression, and an ever more bitter national and religious campaign against the Romans, the Jewish war in its turn brought devastation and disaster.[5] The destruction of the war itself was followed by expropriations. But it is easier to detect the long-term effects of this upheaval on early Christianity than to find extensive evidence of its immediate impact. The sources are generally thought to antedate the fall of Jerusalem. Matthew and Luke seem to reflect a more distant situation and a later period. The destruction of the city may be alluded to in these two gospels, but not in tones which suggest that it was a recent occurrence. Mark is generally dated closest to the period of the revolt, but its precise date, location, and relation to these events is far from self-evident. The apocalyptic discourse in Mark 13 seems to some extent to reflect the need of Judaean Christians to flee to the mountains without stopping to gather up belongings (Mark 13.14–16). Perhaps the pre-Lucan injunction to sell one's garment and buy a sword also belongs to the confusion of this period (Luke 22.36).

In examining the oral tradition of Jesus's teaching on property and riches we shall need to keep these factors in mind. Here and there we may be able to see how the teaching was adapted and amplified in the changing economic circumstances of the early

Church. But we must also ask how much of the oral tradition reflects an earlier situation altogether, namely that of the ministry of Jesus. Here again our information is limited, and dependent on inference from the sources. Yet certain features of the activity of Jesus do emerge from a careful and critical scrutiny of the evidence. There is general agreement that he was a Galilean, baptized by John the Baptist, who travelled the countryside proclaiming the imminent reign of God. His parables challenged his hearers to respond to his proclamation of the coming Kingdom. His teaching seems to have implied that the present situation was already to some extent changed by the onset of the ultimate eschatological drama. Some of his hearers accompanied him on his travels, and were with him when he was arrested and executed in Jerusalem.

An itinerant prophet of an imminent apocalyptic drama is hardly likely to have upheld the values of an age he regarded as all but ended. The eschatological core of Jesus's message is the one thing on which the majority of scholars are agreed. It is here therefore that we shall find, if anywhere, the clue to his attitude to property, to poverty, and to wealth. But we must investigate the texts with care. We must do so with an alertness to the fact that Jesus's teaching seems to have been amplified and adapted in the light of later circumstances. We must also be careful to ask whether Jesus's passionate concern for the future reign of God led to a hatred and depreciation of the things of this world, or a desire and longing for a time when the sick would be healed, the oppressed would go free, and the wrongs of the present would be transformed in a new and better age. We are at present only setting the scene for the more detailed appraisal of individual passages from the texts which must now follow.

REVERSAL OF FORTUNE IN THE COMING AGE

Three main passages will be examined under this heading. These are the woes on the rich and the well fed, the parable of Dives and Lazarus, and the penultimate verses of the Magnificat. These three passages have in common the theme that in the new age God will reverse, or has already begun to reverse, the good fortune of the prosperous.

In examining these passages we need to bear in mind a particular factor. Sociologists tend to regard expectations of this kind as characteristic of the religions of the disprivileged. This sociological approach also notes that in modern society people's hopes may take a secular form: those with few prospects hope that their children will succeed where they themselves have not.[6] But closer to what we are examining at present are studies of the widespread religious hope that present sufferings will merit future compensation. The projection of this hope into a future life is one aspect of the wide range of forms this expectation takes.[7] The hope of a better future maintains a sense of honour and of self-justification. Against a background in which suffering is generally thought to be deserved, the disprivileged maintain their innocence by a strong conviction that their particular sufferings are the result of injustice and will soon be rectified. Undeserved suffering is regarded as meritorious.[8] When the suffering which merits compensation is seen as the result of injustice a further factor may be involved, namely the element of resentment. It may well be that the rich are, or are thought to be, the cause of the sufferings of the disprivileged, and that this suspicion is associated with an expectation of doom and disaster for the rich. In such circumstances belief in divine retribution may be an ill-concealed form of a hope for revenge.[9] Max Weber elaborated this view in relation to Judaism, but it has also been applied to Christian sectarian groups in the medieval and Reformation period, and to modern religious movements.[10] Also within sectarian religion a sense of high religious privilege may serve as compensation for low socio-economic status.[11] A further factor is the suggestion that when prejudiced groups accuse other groups of accumulating worldly riches and seeking to dominate, they may be projecting on to others what they themselves are tempted by and dare not admit.[12] This factor needs to be remembered, although there may often have been actual justification for such accusations in the texts we are considering. The more sophisticated studies have focused attention on the function of *relative* disprivilege rather than disprivilege as such, and on the particular role of socially marginal elements in the composition of 'millenarian' or apocalyptic sects. All this has a bearing on the theology of reversal which is to be found in certain strata of biblical literature.

Examples of reversal theology are common in the psalms where they may often reflect the religious and political aspirations of a small nation at the mercy of powerful neighbouring states and empires. Thus we find in Psalm 147.6:

> The Lord lifts up the downtrodden (*ʿanāwîm*),
> he casts the wicked to the ground

(in a psalm which appears to celebrate the rebuilding of Jerusalem after the exile (147.2) It is in the psalms especially that this motif is found, and references to several further passages have already been noted. Closer to New Testament times are passages from the Admonitions of Enoch, the Psalms of Solomon, and the Qumran Hodayoth from which a few examples may be given.[13] In the Hodayoth we find a simple celebration of deliverance:

> But Thou, O my God, hast succoured the soul of the poor and the needy against one stronger than he ... [1Q Hod. 2.34–5, trans. Vermes.]

In a commentary on the psalms from Qumran we find a prophecy of future reversal:

> Interpreted this concerns the congregation of the Poor, who [shall possess] the portion of all.... They shall possess the High Mountain of Israel ... and enjoy ... delights in His Sanctuary ... the wicked of Israel ... shall be cut off.... [4 QpPs. 37.21–2, trans. Vermes.]

This predicts that the poor sectarians will take over the Temple at present controlled by the Wicked Priest who 'plunders the goods of the poor'. This is reversal theology with a vengeance! The Qumran sectarians would certainly merit classification as a socially marginal group, and seem to have the outlook of such a group. The War Scroll goes further still and predicts that God will 'deliver into the hands of the poor the enemies from all the lands, to humble the mighty of the peoples by the hand of those bent to the dust....' [1Q Mil. 11.13, trans. Vermes.] Here we have religious apocalyptic harnessed to the chariot of violent revolution.

But such motifs are not found universally in Jewish texts. They represent the aspirations of one strand of Jewish piety. Nor are such expectations confined to Judaism. A brief example from the Hellenistic world will make that clear. In the poems of Cercidas, Zeus is asked why he does not take *rich* Xenon and make him the child of *poverty* 'and give to us who deserve it the silver that now runs to waste' (Cercidas fr. 4, trans. J. U. Powell).[14] Here we hear the voice of the poor and oppressed in Greece of the third century B.C. The fact that it is Zeus rather than Jahweh who is invoked should not be allowed to conceal the evident similarity of desire for reversal of fortune, even if in the gospels the reversal is postponed to the hereafter.

Within early Christianity we may find a theology of reversal in James and Revelation. So we find the fate of the rich predicted in James in the following terms:

> Come now, you rich, weep and howl for the miseries that are coming upon you.... (James 5.1.)

The rich in question are accused of withholding wages, living in luxury, and killing the innocent. In Revelation 18.16 the author of the Apocalypse views with evident satisfaction the cries of the wealthy merchants of the now 'destroyed' city which had once been the capital of wickedness and persecution. They cry:

> *Woe, woe*, for the great city that was *clothed in fine linen, in purple* and scarlet.... In one hour all this wealth has been laid waste. [RSV adapted.]

We may now examine in more detail the woes on the rich in Luke 6.24 and the tale of the fiery torment in store for the rich man clothed in purple and fine linen (Luke 16.19–31).

The Woes

> But woe to you that are rich, for you have received your consolation.
> Woe to you that are full now, for you shall hunger.
> Woe to you that laugh now, for you shall mourn and weep.
> Woe to you, when all men speak well of you, for so their fathers did to the false prophets. (Luke 6.24–6.)

Beatitudes and woes occur separately in Jewish tradition, and also occasionally in pairs.[15] Separate beatitudes and woes appear elsewhere in the New Testament generally, as well as in the gospel tradition.[16] But the set of four woes in Luke 6.24–6 are so closely modelled on the preceding beatitudes that it seems unlikely that these woes ever existed apart from the set of four beatitudes which presumably stood in Q. We may for the moment leave open the question of whether individual beatitudes existed separately in the Jesus tradition before forming a group. Certainly the last of the present group of beatitudes reflects a time of hostility towards disciples of Jesus. From that we may reasonable infer that the group of four beatitudes (and four corresponding woes) reflects the situation of primitive Christianity. But we have already given reasons for holding that the woes are pre-Lucan, and perhaps stood in Q.[17] This gives us upper and lower limits for dating the woes. They belong to the period between the time of Jesus and the compilation of sources such as Q. The combination of beatitudes and woes seems to be a prophetic apocalyptic feature.[18] We cannot exclude the possibility that individual beatitudes and woes preceded the set of four plus four, but the close link of the woes to the previous beatitudes makes it unlikely that the woes existed separately. But the woes do seem to disturb the sequence in Luke 6. The teaching on love towards enemies which follows in Luke 6.27 does so awkwardly. The difficulty of the transition has been frequently noted and discussed. The progression would be easier if the injunction to love one's enemies (in Luke 6.27) immediately followed the final blessing on those who undergo reproach for the sake of the Son of Man.[19] This means that the woes may well be an insertion which disturbs the original sequence. But if that is so, they are an insertion into the source prior to the time of Luke. We have already noted that the non-Lucan vocabulary of the woes, and their occasional points of contact with Matthew's beatitudes, point to the pre-Lucan character of the woes.

The argument so far would assign the origin of the woes to the period between the time of Jesus and the compilation and use of sources such as Q. Any attempt to narrow these limits can only be speculative. Yet it is tempting to make such an attempt in the light of the evidence at our disposal. The woes express a theology of eschatological reversal. The rich enjoy their good fortune now, but will weep and lament in the future. Now they are held in honour, but improperly. Now they feast, but in the future they will starve. This hope of reversal has its origin in the piety of oppressed minorities within Judaism, as we have seen.[20] Among the passages from 1 Enoch we might recall:

Woe to you, ye rich, for ye have trusted in your riches,

And from your riches shall ye depart,
Because ye have not remembered the Most High in the days of your riches. [1 Enoch 94.8, trans. R. H. Charles.]

This and other passages from 1 Enoch are rather more explicit about the wickedness of the rich than is the case in Luke 6.24. But the hope of reversal is typical of a sectarian outlook, inspired by a situation of persecution and relative disprivilege.[21] The woes preserved in Luke would seem to belong to a particular period in the development of early Christianity. They describe a situation in which Christians are poor, hungry, miserable, excluded, and abused (Luke 6.20–22). Their opponents are highly regarded, happy, well fed, and rich. Such a situation existed in the early years of Palestinian Christianity, particularly during the famine of *c.* A.D. 47–8. The price of bread rocketed, and many starved. The system of mutual aid in the Jerusalem church proved insufficient, and help eventually came from Christians in Antioch. Aid to the Jewish community came from Adiabene, through the leading men of Jerusalem.[22] But the existence of a separate Christian organization suggests that Christians were unlikely to benefit from the usual Jewish system of relief, which was itself under great strain. This was a time when the rich would have been especially the target for bitter resentment. They were cushioned from hardship by their wealth, and as leaders of the community they were in charge of relief funds unlikely to benefit those who recited the woes. Because of the extensive controversy between Christianity and Pharisaism, the hostility which, in this period, existed between Christians and the wealthy Sadducean aristocracy, has sometimes been underestimated. Acts 4.1 and 5.17 specifically mention the Sadducees as hostile to Christianity, as does Josephus.[23] The woes on the rich may well reflect that hostility, as also the passage which we must examine next.

The Story of Dives and Lazarus (Luke 16.19–31)

This story has long been a source of embarrassment to moralizing interpreters. It seems to justify the poor man, and to condemn the rich man, simply because of their respective poverty and riches. The text does not mention Lazarus's piety, nor does it speak of the godlessness of Dives.[24] Dives's wealth is not castigated as ill-gotten gain, nor is his neglect of Lazarus mentioned in Abraham's reply to him in verse 25. It is true that he and his brothers are portrayed as unrepentant gluttons who ignore the judgement which comes after death. Also his neglect of the poor may be implied in the story, even if the point is not made explicit. There is therefore some warrant for seeing Dives as representing the heedless and 'brutal oriental rich', but the parable does not labour this as much as the commentators on it. The parable certainly gives the fullest description of the rich who are condemned in the gospels. It reflects the fairly sharp division of first-century Palestinian society into rich and poor which we noted in the opening chapter. The rich were very few in number and were chiefly the large merchants and the big landowners. The priestly aristocracy belonged to this class. Though the Pharisees were influential and later became dominant, in this period the rich nobility were mainly Sadducees.[25]

The story is probably from Luke's special source. Its use of historic presents, and some twenty words employed nowhere else in Luke,[26] at least suggest that it is pre-Lucan. It is a double parable, and as in other examples of this form, the emphasis lies on the second half.[27] The parable is therefore shaped as a warning to those who live in present luxury with no thought of what awaits them after death. In this respect it echoes ideas found in 1 Enoch 102–4. There the wicked praise their fellows who 'have died in prosperity and wealth', but they are told that they will 'descend into Sheol ... into darkness and chains and a burning flame' whereas the oppressed righteous are promised 'great joy as the angels of heaven'.[28]

But the story is much older. The motif can be traced back to Egypt some three centuries earlier, and a similar story was told by the rabbis.[29] Jeremias argues that Jesus made use of this Jewish parable of Bar Ma'jan. Part of that Jewish parable certainly has close similarities with the parable of the great feast in the gospels. But whether it was Jesus or his followers who used the rest of the story here remains to be decided. The Jewish story asks why a pious man died unrecognized, while the funeral of Bar Ma'jan the son of a tax collector was observed by the whole city. The answer follows the normal Jewish doctrine of rewards. The pious man had committed one sin (which his mean funeral cancelled); the tax collector's son had done one good deed (which his splendid funeral cancelled). Thereafter the godly man was rewarded, and the other man was tormented with thirst. It is clear that the story of Dives and Lazarus is less concerned with rewards for good deeds, and more with poverty and riches.[30] This causes difficulty for Jeremias who wishes to attribute the story to Jesus. He notes that it appears to teach that wealth itself is punished and poverty is rewarded. 'Where has Jesus ever suggested that?' he objects. But such a view *is* implied by the author of the woes. Here, as there,[31] we find a doctrine of reversal which is simpler and sharper than the teaching of the rabbis, and closer to that of the Admonitions of Enoch. We should also note that Luke 16.31 contains early Christian resurrection apologetic. In view of that, the most reasonable line is to assign this version of the story to the same period as the woes and to see it as reflecting tension between poor members of the early Church and the wealthy Sadducees. The description of the rich man who feasts and does not care about the coming resurrection supports that interpretation.[32]

The story of Dives and Lazarus differs from many of Jesus's parables. It does not describe the imminence of the coming Kingdom by means of a similitude. Instead of that it is a cautionary tale with a description of death and the after-life derived from the popular belief of the time. It probably belongs not to Jesus's parables of the Kingdom, but to early Christian apologetic.[33] This is especially clear from Luke 16.31. The situation is one where an impoverished Christian community find themselves confronted by a wealthy section of Jewish society,[34] which disregards their sufferings and scorns their hope in life after death. Like some of the Jewish sects before them, these Christians look for a reversal of fortunes after death.[35] The outlook is somewhat similar to that found later in James 2.6–7 and 5.1–6.

The parable is clear evidence that one branch at least of early Christianity taught that to live a life of luxury and affluence was incompatible with salvation. The dualism of this story is that of the woes and of the saying about the impossibility of serving both God and mammon. There are further examples in the rest of the New Testament.[36] Jesus certainly taught the pressing need for decision to accept the Kingdom. He and his disciples treated earthly possessions with carefree abandon, and perhaps also saw them as hindrances. Here, though, we see the transformation of a joyful acceptance of the demands of the Kingdom into an attitude of severity and even harsh resentment. This last is the mark of a sect rejected by its parent society, faced with pressing economic need, and hostile to the heedless affluence of the wealthy. Not unnaturally it reacts as other sects, similarly placed, have reacted before and since. If we were to assign the story to a specific period, then the time of the famine would be the most likely.

The Magnificat
(Luke 1.53)

He has filled the hungry with good things,
and the rich he has sent empty away.

At this point it is reasonable to ask whether the Magnificat does not express sentiments similar to those we have examined in the woes and in the story of Dives and Lazarus. In this poem the rich are mentioned along with proud 'dynasts' and contrasted with the humble and hungry of Israel who fear God and are recipients of his mercy. The difference is that the poem, though undoubtedly expressing the hope of reversal, is nominally at least a celebration of the work of God in bringing that reversal about already, or at least beginning to do so. Nor is the poem among the teaching attributed to Jesus. We have contended that an early Christian community produced the woes and saw Jesus in the context of hopes of God's coming reversal of fortune. Such a community would have been happy to adopt this poem from Judaism, or to create it in continuation of the hopes of apocalyptic Jewish sectarians. Though the woes, the story of Dives and Lazarus, and this poem may not belong to one source, they are all transmitted in the material which Luke inherited.

Compensations for Followers of Jesus
(Mark 10.28–30)

Linked to resentment and the hope of reversal of fortune is the expectation of compensation. This we find in the closing section of the passage about riches in Mark 10. This passage echoes the Jewish doctrine of rewards both in this life and hereafter, but here good things are promised to disciples in *both* aeons, though with persecutions in the present. Those who have left home, family, and lands are promised ample return in this life and eternal life thereafter. The first part of the promise presumably reflects the experience of common life in the Church, such as is described in Acts 2–4. In its present form at any rate this seems to be the tenor of the passage.[37] But it is worth noting that in this passage we do not find the converse stated, that those who enjoy present prosperity will later lose it. That element is barely perceptible in Mark. It is perhaps just hinted at in the repetition of the saying that the first will be last and the last first.

In concluding this whole section the following observations seem appropriate. The hope of compensation is found in Mark as well as in the Lucan sources. But the specific expectation of a reversal of fortune hereafter in which the rich suffer and the poor are compensated, is mainly in the passages examined previously. In the case of two of these, the woes and the story of Dives and Lazarus, the *Sitz im Leben* seems to be that of early Christianity suffering poverty, hunger, and derision while others feast and are prosperous. I have suggested the period of the famine as a time when these tensions were most acute.

PASSAGES WHICH CONDEMN HOARDING AND PRAISE GENEROSITY

The next group of passages to be examined are those which either condemn the hoarding of possessions, or urge generosity in a more striking manner than was common at the time. In this somewhat disparate group are included the following passages: on treasures; the story of the rich fool; on not serving both God and mammon; on the camel and the eye of the needle; and the parable of the sheep and the goats. All of these display a direct hostility to the accumulation of wealth or the preservation of such treasure, or else commend generosity. The question to be asked is to what extent these passages reflect the early years of a struggling community in which condemnation of hoarding and praise of generosity was a pressing matter.

On Treasures
(Luke 12.33–4; Matt. 6.19–20, cf. Thomas log. 76b)

The version in Thomas runs:

> You must also seek for the treasure which does not perish, which abides where no moth comes near to eat and no worm destroys. [trans. Metzger.]

The wording of the first part of the synoptic saying differs considerably. Matthew begins: 'Do not lay up for yourselves treasures on earth. . . .' This is both rhythmical and an example of antithetic parallelism,[38] but may be redactional and shaped liturgically.[39] Luke opens with 'Sell your possessions, and give alms; provide yourselves with purses that do not grow old. . . .' This version is also rhythmical, though lacking the antithetic parallelism of Matthew.[40] Thomas has only the middle section about seeking the treasure which does not perish. It could be that this was the original unit, though it does seem that the version in Thomas reflects gnostic interpretation.[41] The context varies. Thomas places the saying after the parable of the pearl. In Matthew it appears in the Sermon on the Mount prior to the passage about 'cares'. Luke normally preserves sayings in their Q context,[42] whereas Matthew seems to have excerpted from, and rearranged, Q. Matthew's variation of opening and placing may possibly reflect his omission of the parable of the rich fool,[43] just as the poetry of his version may reflect his own poetic sensitivity.

The saying probably once appeared in Q as part of a little catechism about fearless confession during persecution, lack of concern for earthly needs, and reward for faithful service (Luke 12.2–46). The saying reflects teaching on almsgiving which is common both to Judaism and to early Christianity. There is nothing in it which would prevent one from attributing it to the teaching of Jesus, but it does not belong to the strikingly new elements in that teaching.[44] The extensive parallels make that clear. The chief themes of the saying are the transitory nature of earthly wealth,[45] the permanence of heavenly treasure,[46] and the contrast between the two.[47] These themes are well known in Judaism, and some of those who have contested this do not seem to have looked very far.[48] The most striking parallel is in T.Pea 4.18 par.,[49] and refers to an incident during the famine of *c.* A.D. 48. King Monobazus (Izates according to Jos. Ant. 20.53) distributed his treasures to the poor. When challenged, he replied:

> My fathers gathered treasures for here below and I have gathered them for above ... my fathers gathered treasures into a place over which hands can gain control. I have gathered treasures to a place where no hand can gain control....

Braun correctly notes that this passage is not typical of rabbinic Judaism,[50] but it is, however, not untypical of one attitude within Judaism. The Jewish version presumably reflects the period of the famine. It could well be that the synoptic version also belongs to that period, and that the sentiment was current at the time. The injunction to sell possessions in order to give alms (Luke 12.33a) is more unusual and perhaps reflects earlier Christian teaching. The Matthean version implies, the Lucan version states, that to give money to others is the way to obtain heavenly treasure. In explicitly demanding the sale of property, Luke 12.33a seems to have in mind situations similar to that described in Acts 4.36–7. Converts like Barnabas who had resources to spare sold them in order to aid the poor within the community. If the saying was uttered by Jesus, then it was perhaps part of an appeal for alms to support an itinerant group of disciples. But the later date seems more likely for this passage.

The Rich Fool
(Luke 12.16–20; cf. Thomas log. 63)

The version in Thomas runs:

> There was a rich man who had many possessions. He said, I will use my possessions that I may sow and reap and plant and fill my storehouses with fruit, so that I may lack nothing. These were his thoughts in his heart. And in that night he died. He who has ears, let him hear. [trans. Metzger.]

The version in Luke differs somewhat in that there the rich fool has accumulated possessions and decides to sit back and enjoy them. The Lucan version is also placed between two interpretative additions (12.15 and 12.21) which are absent in Thomas (though we need not assume that the version in Thomas is older). The additions attack covetousness, greed, and hoarding.[51] They show us how the parable was understood in the tradition.

The story demonstrates how sudden death prevents the enjoyment of accumulated wealth. This is a common theme of popular wisdom and folklore.[52] Jeremias wishes to interpret the parable in an eschatological sense: Jesus likens the coming catastrophe to the sudden death of the rich fool.[53] This reconstruction is speculative, and not very clear from the parable itself, which does seem more concerned with the question of riches. Jeremias has to admit that some emphasis is still placed on the folly of heaping up possessions in the last days. Certainly the point of the story is more than 'the brevity and uncertainty of life'. The purpose of the tale is to expose the folly of hoarding possessions which one may never live to use. The eschatology in question seems to be that of the death of the individual. In this it differs from some of the eschatological parables of Jesus, but it is not incompatible with his teaching. But to whom did the early Christian interpreters of the story apply it? Did they see it as aimed against the rich who stayed outside the new community? Or did they apply it to members of the Church? In spirit, the story is closer to the saying on treasures than to the story of Dives and Lazarus, so it is probably addressed to members of the Church. Despite the exaggerated language about renunciation, and the glowing descriptions of common life in the Church, the reality may have been less heroic, and exhortations against selfish hoarding not uncommon.

'... You cannot serve God and mammon' (Luke 16.13c; Matt. 6.24c)

This saying may well once have been independent of the proverbial passage (about not serving two masters) which precedes it.[54] Thomas has the proverb without the saying which we are discussing.[55] In Matthew and Luke the two are found together, but in different secondary collections of sayings about money. In Matthew they appear in the Sermon on the Mount. In Luke they are part of a group of sayings following the parable of the unjust steward. This latter group is held together by the catchword 'mammon', which only appears here in the New Testament, though it is found in Jewish texts.

The word 'mammon' refers to wealth or property, including

money.[56] It does not refer exclusively to ill-gotten gains.[57] Here the word refers to property or money in a derogatory manner, and half personifies it.[58] It is not only in the gospels that the service of wealth is seen as the service to an idol.[59] The sharp antithesis between God and money is alien to rabbinic Judaism, but similar contrasts are made in many other texts. We find renunciation of the pursuit of wealth in 1QS 9.22 and 10.19, while 1 Enoch 108.8 praises those who 'love God and loved neither gold nor silver. . . .' In Philo fr.II 649 we read: 'It is impossible for love of the world to coexist with the love of God.' A sharp contrast is also made between God and the world in the New Testament epistles (cf. 2 Cor. 6.14–15; James 4.4; 1 John 2.15). The Hebrew Bible does not go so far, but does, of course, contrast God and false deities. Slavery to wealth is a common image in Hellenistic literature,[60] and one passage contrasts covetousness with divine knowledge.[61] Clearly some of these parallels are closer than others, but they show that the sentiment in our text is not particularly novel. The secondary nature of the context adds to the impression that this was a piece of commonplace teaching which could have been included in Q. It is not inconsistent with the teaching of Jesus, and is certainly compatible with a sharp contrast of the values of this present age and the coming Kingdom, but it suits the situation of the Church at least as well as that of the ministry, if not better.

The Eye of a Needle
(Mark 10.23–5 par.)

'. . . it is easier for a camel to go through the eye of a needle than for a rich man to enter the kingdom of God.'

The first task in discussing this passage is to establish the text. There seems to be a certain amount of repetition and redundancy in verses 23–5. Entry into the Kingdom is mentioned three times and the difficulty of entry is twice directly and once symbolically expressed. Some texts (D a b d ff^2) provide verse 24 after verse 25. These and other texts[62] include a reference to the rich, or those who trust in money, in verse 24. But there are further manuscripts which offer verse 24 between verses 23 and 25 and have no reference at all to riches in verse 24. This last group includes ℵ and B as well as other texts.[63] This is the version printed by Nestlé, and the UBS, and translated in the RSV and the NEB. This is probably what Mark wrote, but the reasons for accepting the shorter text in the order verses 23, 24, 25 must now be rehearsed.

The first point concerns the reference in verse 24 to the rich, to those who have money, or to those who trust in money. The texts vary considerably, and some of the better texts lack any such phrase. These last must surely be right. The absence of qualification in verse 24 gave rise to a difficulty which various emendations attempted to resolve. They all attempt to harmonize verse 24 with verses 23 and 25. Matthew and Luke adopted the simpler remedy of omitting the entire verse. We conclude then that verse 24 spoke of a *general* difficulty of entry into the Kingdom, unlike verses 23 and 25 which speak of extreme difficulty for the rich.

But there is still the problem of the order. Some of the Western texts place verse 24 after verse 25. This certainly gives an easier sequence but is suspect for precisely that reason.[64] Further, the opening of Matthew 19.24, 'Again I tell you', seems to echo the 'again' of Mark 10.24. In that case we may conclude that Matthew had before him the order Mark 10.23, 24, 25. The Western text may have changed the order for convenience, or verse 24 could have been overlooked and inserted after verse 25 owing to the similarity of the phrases which are repeated in the passage, and also perhaps owing to familiarity with the sequence in Matthew and Luke which have dropped verse 24 completely, or almost completely.

Yet verse 24 with its general pronouncement: 'Children, how hard it is to enter the kingdom of God!' fits badly into the context. The problem posed by the verse led to the variations in the text. But why does it fit so badly? Wellhausen scented redundancy in the text and wished to delete the reference to the rich in verse 25b. But Matthew and Luke both have the reference to the rich at that point, and no text of Mark lacks it.[65] More recently a different solution has been proposed by Walter[66] and elaborated by Légasse. This is that verse 24b represents the relic of an original saying of Jesus about the general difficulty of entry into the Kingdom. This general saying was similar to Matthew 7.14 par., 'For the gate is narrow and the way is hard, that leads to life, and those who find it are few.' This saying about a general difficulty was then joined to the story of the rich man, and adapted to apply more specifically to the rich. Walter thinks that this adaptation was made by Mark, but there are indications that the complex is pre-Marcan, although Mark may have contributed something. Walter and Légasse may well be correct in seeing verse 24b as the oldest part of the section. In that case verses 23 and 25 import a specific reference to the rich which was made when the complex about riches was compiled. This complex clearly comprises Mark 10.17–22; 10.23–5; 10.28–30. But what do we make of verses 24a, 26, and 27? These express amazement by the disciples and the reply that what is humanly impossible is possible for God. Légasse thinks that this is also part of the oldest unit. It certainly breaks the sequence of 23, 25, and 28–30. The response of the disciples there is that they have given up everything. In verses 26–7 (as also 24a) we meet shock and amazement. This is a familiar motif in *Mark*.[67] Moreover, in addition to the clear echoes of Genesis 18.14, the sentiments in verses 26–7 are very close to early Christian theology. The thought that what is impossible for man is possible for God may well have been intended to console readers of the hard saying against the rich in the previous verses. At least the expressions of surprise seem to represent a Marcan touch, perhaps also the consoling reply of verse 27.

For our purpose the main conclusion which emerges from these observations is that the references to the rich in verses 23 and 25 seem to belong neither to the evangelist nor to the oldest stratum, but to the tradition. It seems to have been qualified by a later expansion expressing surprise. What is more problematical is whether verse 24b represents an earlier version of the saying describing a general difficulty of entry into the Kingdom. If this is so, then when this was linked to the story of the rich man's refusal a further point was added. What was in any case difficult, was supremely so for the rich. The pronouncement in question contains what seems to have been an old Jewish proverb. In the Talmud the performance of impossibilities was similarly described. The saying runs: 'Perhaps you are from Pumpeditha where they draw an elephant through the eye of a needle.'[68] Mark 10.25 states that it is easier for a camel to go through the eye of a needle than for a rich man to enter the Kingdom of God. The text plainly speaks of an impossibility, and all attempts to reduce the camel, or to enlarge the needle's eye, are ridiculous.[69] We need look no further than Luke 6.24 or Luke 14.33 to see the strength of feeling in the gospel tradition on this question.

The pronouncement in question belongs to the category of entry sayings. Judgements were needed about who could, and who could not, enter the community of those eligible for the coming Kingdom. Jesus seems to have invited all alike: rich and poor, righteous and sinners. The tax collectors with whom he consorted were not poor. But this saying limits entry and thereby excludes, or virtually excludes, the rich. No doubt Jesus was aware of the hindrance that possessions placed in the way of entry to the Kingdom, but Jesus's disciples were originally an open group. It was later that the Church took upon itself the task of deciding who did and who did not belong. It saw itself as possessing the power of the keys, and the right to reject applicants or expel erring members. Other examples of such statements are the following:

> Do you not know that the unrighteous will not inherit the kingdom of God? (1 Cor. 6.9.)
>
> ... those who do such things shall not inherit the kingdom of God. (Gal. 5.21.)
>
> ... no immoral or impure man, or one who is covetous (that is, an idolator) has any inheritance in the kingdom of Christ and of God. (Eph. 5.5.)
>
> Has not God chosen those who are poor in the world to be rich in faith and heirs of the kingdom ... ? (James 2.5.)

These and similar passages show how the Church reverted to a more exclusive viewpoint.[70] The idea that the rich as such are excluded differs substantially from rabbinic Judaism, but is here stated with less fierceness than in the Admonitions of Enoch, or the material preserved only in Luke. All the same, it seems to have been sufficiently fiercely stated to evoke the shocked response supplied in verses 24a and 26.

'So therefore, whoever of you does not renounce all his possessions cannot be my disciple.' [My trans.]

On Renouncing Possessions (Luke 14.33)

So far we have explored passages which urge the storing of treasure in heaven and generosity with earthly possessions, which mock those who store up possessions on earth, which say bluntly that one cannot serve God and mammon, and which declare that it is easier for a camel to go through the eye of a needle than for a rich man to enter the Kingdom. Luke 14.33 does not seem so extreme if set in that context. Commentators and others have not been slow to try to attenuate the force of the saying. One of these attempts is to argue for a restricted sense of the word 'disciple' and to claim that only certain members of the early Church, such as those who held special office, were expected to abandon their possessions.[71] This does not seem very convincing, although it was no doubt true that wandering prophets had fewer possessions than more settled members of the early communities. A second approach is to suggest that the verb 'renounce'[72] was not meant to be taken *au pied de la lettre*. But the idea of an inner renunciation which allowed disciples to be actually wealthy belongs to the more sophisticated mentality of Clement of Alexandria. The one attenuation which does have some plausibility is that suggested by Bornhäuser, that by 'possessions'[73] disposable possessions are meant. The reason for giving some assent to this suggestion is that it tallies with what we know of the practice of early Christianity. In time of hardship disciples certainly had little enough to spare. What happened was that those like Barnabas, who had land which he did not require, sold such possessions and contributed to the community's needs. Apostles and wandering prophets may have had no homes for themselves, but other Christians did. Apostles, wandering prophets, and the destitute within the Church did not, or could not, earn, but other Christians must have done so. We can of course suggest that Luke 14.33 is an uncompromising proclamation of an ideal of total destitution. But it seems more likely it is an expansion of the demands made in Luke 14.26–32. Behind it, though, stand the teaching and the activity of Jesus who was an itinerant and who had no possessions. We shall return later to the question as to whether he required such a sacrifice of all his disciples, but we shall do so in connection with the passages about discipleship and the narratives of the calling of disciples.

The Parable of the Sheep and the Goats (Matt. 25.31–46)

The sheer diversity of the teaching in the gospels is well illustrated by this parable. It is likely, as several scholars have argued,[74] that the parable promises salvation to those who unwittingly served 'the Son of Man' by giving aid to his destitute and sometimes imprisoned disciples. Others have rejected this interpretation[75] and see the parable as encouraging Christians to serve the Son of Man by aiding the poor and those in prison. In either case salvation at the final judgement turns on the revelation to those who gave such aid that they had served the Son of Man. In that case the capacity to give alms is presupposed, and almsgiving rather than total renunciation is what is commended here.

But it is probably correct to see 'the least of these my brethren' in Matthew 25.40 as referring to Christians. Certainly this view fits with passages which say that those who accept the disciples accept Jesus (Matt. 10.40). In that case the parable throws considerable light on the social and economic circumstances of some of the early Christian communities. The members of the new movement suffer poverty and persecution. Others extend to them the charity urged in Isaiah 58.7 and in Judaism generally.[76] This means that the list of sufferings may reflect regular teaching about works of love. Still the description includes hunger, thirst, homelessness, nakedness, illness, and imprisonment. Such were the misfortunes of the poor in the Ancient Near East, and such were the sufferings of itinerant Christian missionaries and impoverished members of more settled but despised and sometimes persecuted communities. But behind this more specific situation lies the general conviction of Judaism and elsewhere that the poor and the weak are especially the objects of God's concern and protection.[77]

THE ORAL TRADITION AND ITS SOCIAL AND HISTORICAL SETTING

The first group of passages in this chapter expressed the hope of recompense, and expected a future reversal of fortune. It was suggested that this issue became particularly acute at the time of the famine. The second group of passages is more disparate. Some contain a critique of selfish hoarding. These use traditional or proverbial teaching to mock the heaping up of earthly possessions, demand a choice between God and mammon, and illustrate the impossibility of the rich gaining entry to the Kingdom. Further passages speak of the renunciations and hardships which many early Christians endured. These passages need to be read in the light of the social and economic circumstances of early Christianity. There is of course much in these passages which is not incompatible with what we know of the teaching of Jesus, although certain features fit the situation of the Church slightly better. If we are to find the ultimate origin of the teaching about the dangers of wealth in the teaching of Jesus, then we need to pursue our investigation into those elements of the tradition which express especial concern for the sufferer, the outsider, and the poor, and into those passages which describe, directly or indirectly, the itinerant ministry of Jesus and his closest followers.

FOUR

Poverty and the Kingdom of God: Jesus and his Disciples

In this chapter we shall still need to bear in mind the attitude of early Christianity to property and wealth, but we must attempt more vigorously to establish what was the teaching of Jesus on that subject. With that end in view we shall consider the blessings on the poor, the rules for wandering Christian preachers, and passages which describe the calling of disciples and their way of life. We first reconsider the beatitudes.

The beatitudes

> Luke 6.20: 'Happy are you who are poor, for yours is the kingdom of God.' Cf. Matt. 5.3: 'Happy are the poor in spirit. . . .' Thomas log.54: 'Happy are the poor, for yours is the kingdom of heaven.' [My trans.]

The discussion of the redactional work of Matthew at an earlier point[1] has cleared the path for a consideration of the earlier form of the beatitudes. Matthew lacks, or probably omitted, the woes which appear in Luke 6.24–6. In their place he offers additional beatitudes. In spite of the undoubtedly Semitic flavour of Matthew's 'poor in spirit', it reflects the moralizing interest which pervades the Matthean redaction in general, and the Matthean beatitudes in particular.[2] In including, or creating, blessings on the meek, the merciful, the pure in heart, and the peacemakers, the particular concern of Matthew is clear. The same is true of the expansion of the original four beatitudes which Matthew shares with Luke.[3] In this connection it is essential to examine the entire set of beatitudes, and not individual units in isolation.

The four woes which match the four beatitudes have also been examined earlier. There it became clear that these are almost certainly older than the Lucan redaction and may well have appeared in the same source as the four beatitudes common to Matthew and Luke.[4] The source which contained the four beatitudes (and probably also the four woes) presumably inherited them as a unit from a time when the early Christians suffered hatred, exclusion, and revulsion (Luke 6.22) as well as poverty, hunger, and misery (Luke 6.20–21).

But the question which must now be considered is whether a distinction is to be drawn between the first three beatitudes and the fourth. The final beatitude reflects a time of hostility or even persecution (Matt. 5.11). Also in Matthew's version the final beatitude is in the second person while the rest are in the third person. Further, the Gospel of Thomas has beatitudes on the persecuted and the hungry (log. 68–9) in another place not alongside the blessing on the poor (log. 54). Opinions vary on the question of the dependence of Thomas on the Synoptic Gospels,[5] but the possibility that the beatitudes once existed separately needs to be considered. It could be the case, as some have argued, that the first three Lucan beatitudes are older than the fourth.[6]

The fourth beatitude is longer than those which precede it. It seems to envisage a time of persecution, or at least of hostility and opposition. And additionally in Matthew it is cast into the second person whereas the remainder are in the third person. Luke has all the beatitudes in the second person and commentators are divided over whether this is the original form.[7] Yet neither the change of person in Matthew, nor the fact that the last beatitude is longer, necessarily show that the final beatitude is later than the others. Daube has listed examples from Jewish liturgy which give a series of blessings in the third person, followed by a longer blessing in the second person.[8] In this respect Matthew is similar to the Jewish liturgical pattern. But even if we accepted the Lucan direct address as earlier, the longer final beatitude is not alien, but a normal conclusion to the series. The four common beatitudes certainly, therefore, form a unit, and we need not *necessarily* conclude that a later fourth beatitude was added to an original three. This set of four offers consolation to Christians at a time when the primitive Church suffered poverty, hunger, grief, and hostility. In this respect the pre-Lucan set of beatitudes is, like the woes, in continuity with a certain tradition of piety within Judaism. As in the Psalms, and in the Qumran texts and elsewhere, the community saw itself as the community of those in actual poverty and need, who looked to God for recompense, and are assured of that trust being rewarded when God's reign comes.[9]

Yet even if some of the arguments for an earlier group of three beatitudes proved inconclusive, it is still open to question whether the first three beatitudes existed singly or as a group. Certainly one or more of the first three could have been spoken by Jesus.[10] In so far as they promise the Kingdom to the poor and the hungry, they are quite compatible with the message of Jesus. He offered the Kingdom to outcasts such as the tax collectors, and to sinners, to the sick, and to the poor. What seems characteristic of his message is the lack of limitation placed on those to whom he offered the hope of the new age which was dawning. That the poor and the hungry should have been included in his concern seems inescapable. His itinerant ministry also to some extent placed Jesus among the poor, and in dependence upon others (see below).

'The poor have good news preached to them' (Matt. 11.5; Luke 7.22)

The passage describes how disciples of John the Baptist question whether Jesus is 'the coming one', and are given the answer that the sick are being healed, and the poor are the recipients of good news. The answer implies that Jesus is the expected deliverer by stating that already the prophecies are being fulfilled. We are probably to see here allusions to Isaiah 35.5–6 and to Isaiah 61.1. These mention the healing of the blind, the deaf, the lame, and the dumb,[11] and the preaching of good news to the poor and humble.[12] The cleansing of lepers and the raising of the dead is not mentioned in these passages but reference could be made to further passages in the Hebrew Bible such as 2 Kings 5; Isaiah 26.19; 1 Kings 17.22; and 2 Kings 4.34. Jewish teaching certainly expected an end to sickness, death, and poverty in the new age.[13] In the Ancient Near East the blind, the deaf, and the lame often had to beg for their living.[14] The good news for the poor is therefore similar to the healing of the afflicted, and means an end of present suffering.

Behind the word 'poor' used in the Q passage under discussion lies the Hebrew text of Isaiah 61.1. The word used there could be translated 'humble', and could refer either to humility of outlook, or humility of status, or both. The best guide to the meaning in such cases is the context, and it is clear from the context, both in Isaiah 61 and in the synoptic tradition, that real affliction is envisaged. The association of the poor with the blind, the lame, the lepers, and the deaf makes this clear. Rabbinic Judaism expected piety to be rewarded in this life and in the coming age.[15] But here we have the promise that the suffering and afflicted are being, and will be, recompensed or restored. Judaism certainly taught and teaches the importance of generosity to the poor and the afflicted, though poverty and sickness were in some texts regarded as a punishment for sin. The gospels show Jesus as rejecting this latter view (Luke 13.2; John 9.2–3). That would fit with the expectation that those who suffer now are to be delivered in the new age which is already dawning. Luke 7.22 par. is saying that, with the coming of Jesus, deliverance is already being achieved, not by natural means, but by the coming of God's reign. The passage is close to the hopes of the psalms and of apocalyptic Judaism in this respect,[16] though differing from them in declaring that the expected deliverance is already inaugurated.

But where is this passage to be located in the history of the tradition? Two periods must be considered: the time of the early Church and the time of Jesus. If we assign this passage to the Church then we would need to see it as part of a continuing desire to clarify the relationship between John and Jesus. The passage contains an implicit Christology which is presumably very early, and commends that Christology by appealing to the fulfilment of prophecy in the healing work of Jesus. In such a context the poor who receive the good news are presumably the members of the community, who see themselves as heirs of the promises in Isaiah 61. Certainly the early Christian community was sometimes referred to as 'the poor', and there was precedent for this use of the terminology of the Hebrew Bible at Qumran.[17]

But many scholars have preferred to trace the origin of this passage to the ministry of Jesus, and this view of the reply to John is widely accepted. So for example Bultmann noted that it is distinguished from Judaism by the 'immediacy of eschatological consciousness', and from Christianity because it lacks explicit Christology, but contains 'Jesus's self-consciousness coming to expression'.[18] Jesus was known as a healer even by his opponents, and the message that the long-expected reign of God is now already transforming the present order is here linked to the healing activity of his ministry. With this we could compare the similar outlook of the Beelzebul controversy in which the exorcisms of Jesus are seen as a sign that the Kingdom of God has already taken people by surprise (Matt. 12.28; Luke 11.20, cf. Mark 3.26). The healing stories of the gospels and the reply to John agree in seeing the afflicted as especially the recipients of the activity of Jesus in this connection. Characteristic of Jesus's ministry is his willingness to go to the outcasts of the society of his country and his time.[19] The proclamation of good news to the poor is part of the insistence that no one is excluded from the invitation to the Kingdom.[20]

The Mission Charge
(Mark 6.8–9; Matt. 10.9–10; Luke 9.3–4, cf. Luke 10.4)

'... take nothing for the journey ...' (Mark 6.8a) [My trans.]

Once again we must start by examining the significance of these rules for wandering preachers in the context of the early Church, and then see if behind that it is possible to detect characteristics of the period of Jesus's ministry. The mission charge is one of those passages preserved both in Mark and in Q. Double attestation of this kind means that the material in question is certainly older than either source. That places it early in the development of the tradition. Indications of a Palestinian environment, which are especially strong in Matthew 10.5–6, also suggest that some at least of the teaching here belongs to the early phases of Palestinian Christianity.

The existence of the Q version has to be inferred from the fact that Luke has two versions of these instructions, and that Matthew and Luke agree against Mark on several points. Luke 9.3–4 is chiefly dependent on Mark 6.8–9. The further account in Luke 10.4 presumably comes from the version supplied by Q.[21] Matthew usually conflates what he takes from Mark with excerpts from Q, whereas Luke tends to keep his sources separate. Luke often omits one version where double traditions exist but in this case we have two versions, one in a Marcan context in Luke 9, the other in a Q context in Luke 10. Matters may not be quite so simple as they appear, however, and Luke 10.4 may be influenced by Mark, just as Luke 9.3 may contain traces from Q.

Instructions for travelling preachers were an important issue for the early Church, and we find debate on the issue in a wide variety of sources, such as 1 Corinthians 9.14, 2 John 10–11, and Didache 11–13. Apostles and prophets travelled from place to place and it proved necessary both to provide for their needs, and to ensure that they neither appeared to be, nor actually were, charlatans. The Didache allows for a stay of two days, or three at the most, but considers a request for a meal or for money the sign of a false prophet.[22] The manner and scope of its mission was a subject to which the nascent Church gave a good deal of attention. The mission charge provides both a justification for mission and rules for its conduct. One can trace different emphases in the different versions, and in Matthew there is greater elaboration and expansion.[23]

The instructions which seem to be common to Mark and Q are these:

1 To travel in pairs (Mark 6.7, cf. Luke 10.1)[24]
2 To take the minimum of equipment (Mark 6.8–9; Luke 10.4)
3 To stay in one lodging in any one place (Mark 6.10; Luke 10.7)
4 To heal, and to deliver the message (Mark 6.7,11; Luke 10.9)
5 To shake the dust off their feet if rejected (Mark 6.11; Luke 10.10–11).[25]

In their present form these instructions clearly reflect the practice of early Christian mission. In fact the third rule presupposes a stay of some duration, during which erring emissaries might be tempted to look for more attractive lodgings.[26] Our concern is especially with the rules about taking minimal equipment, and with the meaning and origin of these instructions. There is variety of detail at this point. Money is forbidden in both sources, as is a bag or wallet used for carrying food or as a begging bag. Q forbids staff and sandals, while Mark forbids the taking of food or extra clothing, but allows a staff and the wearing of sandals. The prohibition of greetings on the journey appears only in Luke 10.4 but is perhaps in keeping with the rest. An exact reconstruction of Q is never something that can be made with complete confidence.

Bag, staff, and sandals were the regular equipment for travellers, whether rabbis or Cynic wandering philosphers.[27] The latter used the bag for begging, and the staff was an obvious protection. To go without a bag meant that one was dependent entirely for food on what was provided at the moment. The lack of money and of a purse in which to put money also enhances this state of helpless dependence and marks out the missionary as different from either an ordinary traveller or a beggar. The lack of staff presumably signified defencelessness, trust, and peacefulness of purpose.[28]

The forbidding of sandals poses a more complicated question. The suggestion that it was a spare pair of sandals which was forbidden may be dismissed, unless it can be shown that taking two pairs was the normal practice. Nor need too much notice be taken of those who wax eloquent about the warm climate. The concession which we find in Mark may be due to the great length of the journeys undertaken in the Gentile mission. Perhaps also, in that environment, the absence of a staff would not have held quite the same symbolic significance as in Palestine during the troubles prior to the revolt. It is hard to imagine that environment alone dictated the Marcan concession, or we would have to ask if outside Palestine the stones were harder, or the dogs more ferocious.

It was rabbinic practice to go barefoot on fast days, although that rule was relaxed for longer journeys between towns.[29] Rabbinic sources also mention two other factors which might have a closer bearing on the prohibition of footwear in Q. First, to go barefoot was a sign of poverty.[30] This, rather than fasting or sorrow, would seem to be in keeping with the rest of the rules in the mission charge. But there is a further factor which has often been cited and which may have a bearing on the matter. Rabbinic rules relating to the Temple Mount forbade the carrying of a staff, or wearing of sandals, dust on the feet, or money contained in cloth or bag or moneybelt.[31] The similarity of these rules to those of the mission charge may be no coincidence.

The rule which forbids greetings on the journey is also problematical. It is recorded only in Luke 10.4 but may be part of the old tradition. The most natural interpretation of the rule is that it symbolizes haste. Oriental greetings, like leavetakings (cf. Luke 9.61) could be lengthy affairs. In a time of urgency and crisis it is necessary to dispense with such formalities. The model for this would then perhaps be 2 Kings 4.29 when Elisha sends Gehazi on a lifesaving journey. Certainly haste, swift decision, and abrupt leavetakings seem to have been characteristic of the urgency with which Jesus and his immediate disciples proclaimed the imminence of the Reign of God. Yet it may not be pedantic to object that if haste alone was significant, the absence of footwear would have been a hindrance to this objective. Perhaps the peace greeting of these missionaries had special significance (Luke 10.5–6),[32] and was not to be uttered idly to all who passed by on the road. The rabbis debated whether one should interrupt prayer before God in order to greet someone.[33]

The severity of these rules is striking. It is unlikely that they can simply be ascribed to the reduced circumstances of the Palestinian Church, though that might have some bearing on the matter. Apostles like Paul who had a skilled trade could find work in new places. Former fishermen like Peter, James, and John had less choice.[34] When they established the community in Jerusalem they had little choice except to depend on their converts as 'fishers of men' and 'labourers worthy of their hire'. Thus the practice became established that apostles and others needed to depend on their converts. By Paul's time this was seen as a privilege, and as one which Paul himself wished to renounce (1 Cor. 9.14–15).[35] But Paul was clearly the exception rather than the rule. In the Ancient Near East hospitality was a sacred duty, and itinerant Christian apostles and prophets could expect short-term hospitality from strangers, and perhaps hospitality of longer duration from converts. There may also have been social factors as well as beliefs about the Kingdom, which had a bearing on the practice of mission itself. Missionary movements have been seen by certain sociologists as a response to a situation in which the beliefs of a small group suffer 'disconfirmation' of a central tenet. This gives rise to a state described as 'cognitive dissonance'. A group in this state may not disintegrate, but rather seek to reduce the dissonance by persuading others to share its belief. Thus missionary efforts directed at the majority may be the somewhat surprising outcome of an event which threatens the beliefs of a minority.[36] But our present concern is not so much with cognitive dissonance and the question of motivation as with the manner and means of the early Christian mission.

The rules which we have been examining ensured that the envoys would be distinguished from ordinary travellers, from beggars, and perhaps from wandering Cynic preachers. The latter may not have been familiar in Galilee and Judaea, though Cynic philosophy was undoubtedly known in Gadara in the Decapolis.[37] Wandering Cynic preachers did indeed often either lack, or renounce, all but the minimum of essentials, and stories about the founders of their movement emphasize this point.[38] Later, however, many imitators, beggars, and degenerate adherents made Cynics even more unpopular than in earlier times.[39] There were attempts to distinguish 'genuine' practitioners of Cynic principles from the rest by some writers, but such a distinction was never easy. As far as early Christianity is concerned, similarity to and differentiation from Cynic wandering preachers was more likely to have been an issue in the Gentile mission.[40] But our present concern is with the striking and radical nature of the renunciations made by the earliest Christian wandering preachers and Cynicism was at that point hardly a major consideration.[41]

Without protection, without reserves of money or of food, in evident poverty, and without the time or inclination for idle greeting, the very appearance of these wandering Christian preachers was a prophetic parable. Behind the institutionalized norms of the formal rules, we may still see the outline of a distinct prophetic and charismatic concern with the coming Kingdom. Poverty, dependence on hospitality, and urgency were the marks of this enterprise. Hahn has rightly pointed out that the insistence on the absence of equipment is entirely compatible with Jesus's attitude.[42] Urgency and trust are the keynotes of this prophetic mission. The disciples travel like Temple pilgrims. Perhaps we should take seriously this similarity with Jewish practice on the Temple mount.[43] It may be that the meaning of the surprising instructions we have examined is that the approach of the Kingdom makes the time a holy season, and the whole land a holy place. Such a time would be a time for total trust and total dependence on God.[44] This interpretation is, of course, conjectural and based on inference. If it can be sustained, then we could perhaps argue that those passages we examined earlier, which urge generosity, would have a connection with what we find here. By throwing themselves on to the hospitality of others, Jesus and his disciples displayed their trust that generosity would be shown, and that a positive response to their message would be forthcoming.

On carrying a Purse (and Buying a Sword) (Luke 22.35–6)

We have already noted that this passage reverses earlier rules.[45] In its context in Luke it relativizes and historicizes the rules of the mission charge. But we have already noted indications that the passage is pre-Lucan. If that is really so, then presumably in a time of great upheaval the old rules had to be suspended. No longer could hospitality be expected, and defencelessness perhaps meant grave danger. The remark about selling a cloak in order to buy a sword suggests that there may not have been much to put in the purse. The Lucan version of the passion displays clear uneasiness about the use of a sword in Gethsemane, and the vast majority of texts in the rest of the tradition do not envisage the possession, let alone the use, of such a weapon. So perhaps verse 38 is intended to reject thoughts of a sword. It might be possible to take verse 36 as figurative and as simply heralding a time of danger. But such a solution seems contrived, and it is better to conclude that in a time of great danger the rules about poverty, trust, and defencelessness were revised.[46] The situation immediately prior to the Jewish revolt of A.D. 66 was very different from the period from A.D. 26 to A.D. 50.

The Rich Man's Refusal
(Mark 10.17–22)

Another story recounting the raising of a rich young man and his initiation into the mystery of the Kingdom has been found in an alleged extract from a secret gospel of Mark in a letter attributed to Clement of Alexandria. The chief problems here are whether the letter is a genuine letter of Clement, which is possible, and if so, whether it contains anything more than a second-century gnostic elaboration of Mark.[47] The two areas of uncertainty make it difficult to decide whether the document tells us anything reliable about second-century Christian attitudes to wealth, let alone about the first-century gospel tradition. In view of this the analysis which follows will concentrate on the text of Mark 10.17–22.

The story is part of a complex in Mark dealing with the question of property and riches. That complex is presumably older than Mark, but is made up of what were probably three separate units: this story, the saying about the needle's eye, and the saying about compensation (Mark 10.17–22; 23–7; 28–31). The story of the rich man's refusal has been much discussed,[48] and we must consider the background to the story, its setting in the life of the early Church, and its relation to other teaching about wealth and discipleship in the Jesus tradition.

The Hellenistic background offers few points of contact with this story. It is true that there is a superficial resemblance between wandering Cynic mendicants and itinerant disciples of Jesus, but the resemblance does not go very deep. The Cynics renounced and abandoned their property, if they had any. But they do not seem to have developed a common life even as rudimentary as that of the band of disciples. They were in no way interested in the Kingdom of God or the law of Moses (Mark 10.19). Only in occasional utterances of proverbial wisdom do we find points of comparison between popular philosophy and the gospels.[49]

Normal Jewish rabbinic teaching of a later period limited the amount which the pious should give away, with the sensible observation that generosity should not go so far that one impoverished oneself and then became a burden to others.[50] Though generosity was frequently urged and commended, one was not allowed to devote all one's property. A Gentile might be directed to sell all his possessions and become a proselyte, but such advice was directed at idolatry, not at wealth.[51] The spectacular generosity of 'Monobazus' during the famine is the theme of several passages,[52] but the crisis was severe, the King wealthy, and the reports were perhaps exaggerated. Outside the sphere of rabbinic Judaism we do find examples of the surrender of property. The Maccabean guerrillas abandoned their property, but they did so in order to take up a 'holy war' (1 Macc. 2.28). The severance of ties was necessary for guerrilla warfare, and part of the tradition of charismatic leadership and the holy war.[53] But the warriors were not averse to taking plunder (1 Macc. 4.27; 2 Macc. 8.25). The severance of ties by Jesus and his disciples may have been equally charismatic, and indicative of total commitment in a crisis, but less military. At Qumran new members handed their property over to the community and this is to a certain extent similar to what happened in early Christianity. Yet this practice was obligatory at Qumran, and voluntary in early Christianity, at least according to Acts 5.4. In the early days at Qumran the community was probably poor and insecure, and the sharing of property necessary for survival in a difficult environment. Later that community was more secure and well organized, but may have relaxed its rules about community of goods.[54] But the Qumran community was a remote settlement, a priestly movement which had broken away from the Jerusalem establishment, and there were differences as well as similarities between it and early Christianity.[55] Some of the similarities might be due to the similar social pressures which led poor and persecuted minorities to adopt some kind of sharing, mutual aid, or common life in order to survive.

We must next ask to what extent the story of the rich man's refusal in Mark 10 might reflect the situation of the early Church in Jerusalem. The emphasis on the commandments (Mark 10.19) would fit the situation, but also others. The financial need of that Church, its designation as 'the poor' (Gal. 2.10) and the practice of expecting converts to sell property and hand over the proceeds may well be reflected in Mark 10.17–22. When a man considered allegiance to the Jesus movement, the leaders of the Church may well have questioned him about his observance of the commandments, and, if he had property, about his willingness to contribute to the relief of the poor within the community.[56] The early Church might well have seen in this story a demand to 'follow' Jesus by becoming a Christian, and to 'give to the poor' by imitating Barnabas. Peter and his companions had long since abandoned means of support in Galilee, and the apostles and other poor among the Christian fellowship expected support from those converts with the means to provide it.

In its present form the story of the rich man's refusal reflects known interests of the early Church in Jerusalem.[57] But the story may well also recall details of an incident in the ministry of Jesus. It is quite likely that Jesus did invite another promising candidate to join the group which followed him. It is later in the tradition that we find a tendency to limit the number of that group. The man is portrayed as a suitable candidate. He has kept the commandments, and is eager to know what needs to be done. Jesus's initial response is entirely favourable (Mark 10.21). The point of the story is the surprise at the end. This point is lost if, with the Gospel of the Hebrews, or with many subsequent moralizing commentators, one tries to turn the man into a villain.[58] It is only when confronted with a demand which goes beyond the ordinary limits of morality that the man draws back. He is invited to join a group of wandering disciples,[59] and it is quite possible that he was asked not simply to abandon his possessions but to dispose of them, and give the proceeds away. What he was asked to do was not so different from what was asked of the other disciples of Jesus. The question at issue is whether Jesus expected only some of his hearers to do what was expected of these disciples.[60] It is important here to distinguish the strata of the tradition. The early Church may well have treated this story as normative, but in a different sense. In the context of Jesus's ministry, not all his hearers became wandering disciples, and he may not have expected all of them to do that. But Jesus certainly proclaimed to all the imminent coming of the Reign of God. It is impossible to eliminate that element, and still make sense of the urgency which permeates the parables and much else. Jesus urged a prompt decision to accept his message of the Kingdom, and the severance of any ties which might stand in the way of accepting that invitation. He spoke and acted as he did because he expected divine irruption, and the transformation of history.[61] If the coming Kingdom is already transforming the present, and calling all existing values into question, then it is hardly surprising to find that someone is urged to sell his property and give the proceeds away. The parables promise the Kingdom, but they also contain demands radical in character and requiring decision. They must not be interpreted in a manner so general as to evacuate their call for decision of specific content. Modern studies of the parables have done valuable work in showing that the parables demand decision for the Kingdom. But *what precisely* did Jesus expect his hearers to do?

Jesus's attitude to possessions does seem to have been radical. He cared little for them. He and his disciples abandoned such things. In this respect we may be able to gain insights into the period of his ministry even though this story was perhaps understood somewhat differently in the early Church.[62] One sees the strength of Percy's case when he contends that Jesus regarded riches as incompatible with participation in the Kingdom. He argues that renunciation (Mark 10.21) is the answer to the question about how to obtain eternal life.[63] The question is whether Jesus expected all his hearers to become wandering charismatics. Clearly some did, and left behind their home and family, perhaps totally and irrevocably in expectation of a new order of things in the Kingdom. This group probably exceeded twelve in number. But not all Jesus's hearers followed him in the literal sense, though his teaching can hardly have offered much comfort to those wedded to the values of an age whose imminent end was being heralded.

THE CALL OF SIMON AND ANDREW, JAMES AND JOHN (Mark 1.16–20)

There are in the gospel tradition very diverse descriptions of the call of the first disciples. One of these scenes even appears in Luke at the beginning of the ministry and in the Fourth Gospel as a post-resurrection narrative.[64] The interest in John 1.41 is largely christological. Here, in Mark, the interest of the narrative is the nature of Christian discipleship. A simple amalgamation of details from the different accounts is therefore inappropriate, and the interests and character of each need to be studied with care. Thus while Taylor primarily sought historicity here, Bultmann described the narrative as a typical scene, and Pesch as an aetiological legend concerned with discipleship.[65] What we have here is more than a mere record of the past, though it may well include reminiscences from the ministry of Jesus. In any case what is recorded is an interpreted and abbreviated version of something which probably took place over a period of time. We are not told whether the disciples had met Jesus previously, or what might have led up to the call and their response to it. The emphasis is placed on the abrupt initiative of Jesus in making the summons, and the equally abrupt acceptance of the call to follow him.[66]

The background to these stories of abrupt summons and response is interesting. We find stories of this kind not only in Mark but also in Q.[67] There too there is an emphasis on the unconditional and immediate severance of ties with the past. This immediately suggests that such a view of discipleship belongs early in Christian tradition, as both Mark and Q attest it. The unmistakable Jewish background also points in the same direction. There is a clear similarity between these stories and the story of the call of Elisha in 1 Kings 19.19–21. Jesus and his disciples are seen in the light of the legends about the charismatic prophets of the Hebrew Bible.[68] We have already noted the role of wandering prophets and apostles in early Christian history, and these narratives serve to explain, commend, and justify such an institution. The concept of the charismatic prophet played an important role both in the later development of Christian asceticism[69] and in the early stages of Christology. The expression 'fishers of men' picks up a metaphor used in Jeremiah 16.16, and at Qumran, and also in the Hellenistic world. It is also possible to see the variation between Mark 1.17 and Luke 5.10 as due to differing translations of an Aramaic version.[70]

It is not always easy to decide on the placing of a saying. The idea that the disciples should be fishers of men was obviously practised in the early days of the Church. Much of the evidence suggests that it was after Easter that the real mission began. Certainly it is at the end of the gospels that one finds the instruction to evangelize, and it is at that point that vigorous missionary activity is sociologically understandable.[71] It was then that the stark alternative was posed, and the disciples did in the end not resume their life as fishermen in Galilee, but became fishers of men for the new faith. In this connection it is interesting to note the evidence in Matthew and in John 21.3 of post-resurrection episodes in Galilee. The mission charge in Q may not have had a setting in the context of the ministry. It is Mark 6 which places the mission of the disciples in that context.

But it is clear from the parables that there was a real mission on the part of Jesus, which preceded the mission of the Church. It is the difference between Jesus's proclamation of the Kingdom and the message of the Church, which establishes the historicity of the former. The difference does not mean total discontinuity, however, and the important factor is that Jesus's message both differed from, and is the necessary presupposition of, the activity of the early Church. It is also hard to avoid the impression of historical accuracy from the many factors which suggest that the ministry of Jesus was an itinerant one, and that his disciples accompanied him, and presumably participated in his itinerant mission.[72] There was a mission before the mission, and it is not simply all to be seen as retrojection from the time of the Church.

The character of Jesus's ministry arose from his conviction that the Reign of God was imminent, and that its coming must be announced throughout the land. It is from this necessity that the itinerant nature of his ministry came about. Analogies from other movements may therefore help a little, but do not fully explain the way in which Jesus and his disciples abandoned family, and home, and previous occupation. It is indeed possible to find a similarly abrupt change in the case of charismatic military leaders, such as the leaders of the Maccabean revolt or the Zealot leaders. Analogies can also be drawn from the sudden decision of others in the ancient world to turn to philosophy, or to take up the serious study of the Torah. But none of these offers an exact parallel.[73] In the case of those who took up the Cynic way of life, it was often financial ruin or exile which made a man turn to philosophy. It may have been the former with Diogenes; it was certainly the latter with Dio Chrysostom. But we simply lack sufficient evidence to examine the social pattern in all such cases. In any event Jesus was neither Zealot, nor Cynic philosopher, nor rabbi. The closest analogies are to be found in the stories about the prophets, and in accounts of Galilean charismatics.[74] There were ascetics such as Bannus, mentioned in Josephus Vita 11, and also, of course, John the Baptist. But Jesus was also distinguished from John the Baptist precisely by a lack of thoroughgoing asceticism (Matt. 11.18–19 par.). Jesus and his disciples abandoned family, home, and possessions, but though at times they may have suffered hunger (Mark 2.23–8), they were not renowned for fasting (Mark 2.19).

Behind the apostolic lack of means of livelihood, the wandering missionaries of the early Church, and the sacrifices expected of other church members, these stories point back to a situation in the ministry of Jesus. Jesus and his disciples left behind possessions and kin. The closest analogies to this renunciation of property are in the prophetic and charismatic tradition, though Jesus and his first disciples were not thoroughgoing ascetics. The imminence of the Kingdom, and the necessity of proclaiming it throughout the land were what brought about the radical abandonment of property and ties. But we must examine further passages, before inquiring more closely into the character of this requirement of the Kingdom.

The Calling of the Four Disciples (after a miraculous catch of fish) (Luke 5.1–11)

This story is clearly a variant of the version which we have just discussed. Luke presumably obtained it from some other source. It has unmistakable affinities with the story in John 21.1–11, thus posing the problem about whether it is really a pre- or post-resurrection story.[75] Though the emphasis on leaving *everything* may be part of the Lucan editing, there is no reason to doubt that here we have a parallel version recounting a radical renunciation by the first disciples of their old way of life.[76]

The Call of Levi
(Mark 2.13–17)

At first this narrative seems to be similar to the stories about Peter and Andrew, and James and John. But Mark never mentions Levi again. Matthew 9.9–13 provides what is basically the same story, but the tax collector is there called Matthew. This makes him a member of the twelve, and so indicates that he did join the wandering group of disciples. That may already be implied in Mark 1.14. What has intrigued commentators is the mention of a party in 'his house', in Mark 2.15. Some think that the house in question was Jesus's home. Nineham suggests that the story originally meant this,[77] even though Mark implies that the house belonged to Levi. Others conclude that Levi was the host, and that he still owned a house.[78] If one were to argue simply on the level of historicity one might think that disposing of a house could take a little longer than discharging oneself from employment as a tax official. One might also guess that Peter abandoned his house but did not perhaps dispose of it, if he left behind an extended family (Mark 1.29–31), which included a wife who later accompanied him on his travels (1 Cor. 9.4–5). One could speculate that if Levi was indeed the host, according to Mark 2.15, then the meal might have been a farewell party, but this is certainly not stated in the text. Most members of the early Church continued to have houses to live in; it was wandering prophets and apostles who depended on the hospitality of others.

But all these speculations suffer from two major difficulties. First, the text says nothing about home *ownership*. Second, Mark 2.15–17 may well be a different story altogether, only linked with 2.13–14 by the mention of tax collectors. The only sure conclusions we can draw from Mark 2.13–14 is that Levi is recorded as having left his work to follow Jesus. It could even be argued that this action resulted from the nature of his work. The story is set in Galilee, so presumably Levi was a tax official under Herod Antipas. Galilee only came under direct Roman rule later. Tax collectors were regarded as thieves and their money as stolen property.[79] Yet though the story cannot be taken as a definite instance of total renunciation and discipleship, we should probably still interpret it in the light of the other stories of this nature.

On Discipleship
(Luke 9.57–60; Matt. 8.19–22 and also Luke 9.61–2)

Matthew has a parallel to two of these three pronouncement stories which appear in Luke 9. This suggests that they may all come from Q. Luke places these stories before the mission charge to the seventy. As Luke is thought to preserve the sequence of Q most of the time, this suggests that these stories preceded the mission charge in Q also.[80] In that case they formed a prelude to the rules for early Christian mission. This tells us about their use in the Church, but does not preclude the possibility of historicity. The stories in question are very brief; they give the barest of details, merely setting the scene for the pronouncement in question. No detail is supplied which could not be inferred from the sayings. As is often the case with pronouncement stories, the sayings may have a greater claim to authenticity than the setting. The incidents provide answers to factors which might deter Christian missionaries. They must leave home, and parents, and family, and travel without prearranged lodging.

(*a*) 'Foxes have holes, and birds of the air have nests; but the Son of man has nowhere to lay his head.'
Bultmann's conjecture that the saying could have circulated independently of its context[81] might be supported by Thomas log. 86, although of course one must always allow for material in Thomas being derived from the Synoptics. The reference to the Son of Man here could well be a product of Christian theology,[82] or else the phrase 'the son of man' could represent an earlier reference to humanity in general. In the latter case an old proverb might have been turned into a saying of Jesus. But the adoption of a somewhat banal proverb would require a reason. The alternative is that the phrase 'the son of man' is a periphrasis for the first person singular. Some think that the saying speaks of persecution or rejection.[83] But it is not imperative to assume that the homelessness of Jesus was due to rejection. Movement was a necessary feature of his ministry.[84] It was the itinerant nature of the ministry of Jesus and his disciples which provided the model for later missionary activity. The saying which follows provides surer evidence.

(*b*) 'Leave the dead to bury their own dead.'
This is so distinctive and uncompromising a saying that many find

more difficulty in accepting its blunt meaning[85] than its authenticity. Bultmann attributed it to Jesus; Fuchs did not include it among his 'persecution sayings'; and Hengel observes that it can hardly be ascribed to Judaism or to church tradition.[86] With its sharp rejection of sacred obligations, it has been held to contain a distinctive claim by Jesus to special authority as the one who announces the nearness of the Reign of God. It does stand close to sayings which place loyalty to the Kingdom above family ties (Mark 3.31–5; Matt. 10.34–7 par.), though these may have undergone expansion. Here it is a sacred obligation to the dead which this saying overrides. The renunciation of family ties, of sacred obligations, and of possessions, all seem to be characteristic of Jesus's message about the coming Reign of God.

(*c*) 'No one who puts his hand to the plow and looks back is fit for the kingdom of God.'
This saying is similar in spirit to those which precede it. What was probably once a proverb is used to urge renunciation in a time of crisis.[87]

Both Mark and Q, therefore, contain stories which set out the character of discipleship. These were used in the Church, perhaps with general application to all Christians, and with more specific reference to those who were to be wandering prophets and apostles. The stories emphasize the severance of ties by those who are to follow Jesus, and they draw on the stories of the charismatic prophets in the Hebrew Bible to do this. But again and again we have suggested that behind the use of these motifs in the early Church lies the urgent and itinerant proclamation of the Kingdom by Jesus and his followers during his ministry. Thus behind the economic problems of the famine and the economic hardships of the earliest community we find something rather different. This is the overwhelming importance for Jesus and for the earliest community of the imminence of the Reign of God. It is the Kingdom which calls all other values into question, and sets aside the ties of other obligations and of possessions.

What is both relevant and necessary here is a study of the connection between Jesus's proclamation of God's Reign, and his and his disciples' attitude to possessions. The parables of the treasure and the pearl offer an opportunity to focus on this particular issue.

The Parables of the Treasure and the Pearl (Matt. 13.44–6) (cf. Thomas log. 109 and 76)

These parables appear in the special Matthean tradition, which we have already noted to have placed less emphasis on renunciation of property than the other sources. If we find renunciation required in material from such a source, then it is very likely that we are dealing with traditional material, much older than the source itself. The Matthean tradition is not devoid of hard sayings, and we must not press this argument too far, but the observation needs to be made.

Whether Thomas provides independent attestation of the parables is hard to assess. Thomas log. 76 speaks of a merchant who finds a pearl, sells his merchandise, and buys the pearl. Jeremias[88] thinks that 'he sold the merchandise' in Thomas is original, and that Matthew has heightened this to 'he sold all that he had' under the influence of Matt. 13.44. But it is unlikely that it is Matthew who heightened this motif, and the antipathy of Thomas to trade needs to be remembered (cf. log. 64 end). The story of the buried treasure in Thomas log. 109 is closer to current folktales.[89] Thomas log. 8 describes a man who catches a large fish, and is content to throw small ones back into the sea. The concern in the versions in Thomas is probably with gnostic revelation or the gnostic elect,[90] but it is possible that Thomas has preserved features which come from an independent line of tradition.

The interpretation of the parables is a matter of long-standing and notorious complexity. In the Matthean version the men who find the treasure and the pearl sell everything in order to obtain them. In Thomas log. 76 it is merchandise which is sold, but the point is similar. The picture offered in the parable is that of a man who is suddenly presented with an opportunity[91] to possess something of great value, and who disposes of previous assets in order to obtain it. In the interpretation of the parable is the emphasis to be placed on the suddenness,[92] or the value[93] of the Kingdom, or on the sacrifice,[94] risk,[95] or investment made by the hearer? Is the emphasis to be placed on the joy which is evoked,[96] or on the commitment[97] which follows?

For our inquiry, the question at issue is this. There is undoubtedly emphasis on the opportunity, whether sudden, valuable, joyful, or all of these together. Is there also in the real situation, to which the parable points, a demand which follows the promise? If so, what is the demand? It is hard to limit some of the parables rigidly to one point. Certainly here most interpreters hold that the parable does make a demand, even if this demand is subordinate to the opportunity. This tallies with the message of Jesus generally, which consists of promise and demand, not one without the other. But what is the demand? One cannot necessarily press the imagery and say that the requirement is to sell everything. But the parable does suggest that all other goods and values must be put at risk, where the attainment of the Kingdom is at stake.

Various attempts have been made to find interpretations which alter or minimize this element of risk or sacrifice. Glombitza proposed that the parable of the pearl is really concerned with the action of God in giving up all to win those whom he loves. This is ingenious, but hard to sustain.[98] Fuchs wrote at some length, and very obscurely, about the interpretation of these parables. His argument seems to be that they call for faith or trust rather than for sacrifice or renunciation.[99] The theological interest becomes clear, when he argues that what is called for on man's side is a non-action, not a work or a deed. But this interpretation attains an astonishing level of virtuosity when he claims that the image 'says the opposite of what is meant . . . it expresses activity instead of rest'.[100] Even Paul was less 'Pauline' than this, and was prepared to speak of faith in terms of renunciation of former advantages for the one thing of supreme worth (Phil. 3.7–8). Other modern interpreters have argued that the two parables do demand total renunciation, but only from disciples.[101] Others again assume a wider audience, but a less specific demand.[102]

The possibility that Jesus did demand renunciation from all should not be dismissed too hastily. It is true that Matthew's version lays greater emphasis on this point than the parallels in Thomas. But it is presumably not Matthew who is responsible for this, though we do find hard sayings in pre-Matthean tradition (e.g. Matt. 5.29–30; 19.10–12). There is an element of demand in the message of Jesus, although that demand is not clearly expressed in these parables, and the word 'demand' requires some qualification. Jesus's message is first and foremost a positive presentation of the imminent coming of the Reign of God as a new era and a new order of things. But that positive promise also has its obverse.

All previous values are called in question by the coming Kingdom. The parables of the Kingdom offer something of supreme worth, compared with which all previous material and spiritual assets lose their value. Possessions, property, the sacred ties of family or religion, the Mosaic law itself, all pale into insignificance beside it. Jesus and those close to him not only placed these things at risk, but discarded many of them. These parables make it clear that it is the joy of discovering the thing of supreme worth which evokes that response.[103] It is, therefore, far from improbable that these parables expect a similar response from a wider audience.

This aspect of the origin of the movement inaugurated by Jesus and his disciples, inevitably invites comparison with other apocalyptic and 'millenarian' movements.[104] In some cases these are derivative from Christianity in one way or another, but in some instances a historical connection with Christianity is minimal or even quite improbable. What should certainly be remembered is that it is not only in the pages of the New Testament that one meets a charismatic leader who challenges accepted authority in a time of crisis, is opposed to concern for property and possessions, yet prepared to receive gifts, and who leaves behind him a problem of adaptation to everyday routine.[105] What is important is to note both those elements that primitive Christianity shares with other apocalyptic movements, and also those features which set it apart.

In his conclusions at the end of a study of modern messianic cults, Lanternari distinguishes the transcendental nature of Christianity from those messianic movements which strive for human salvation on earth. Lanternari goes on to say that Christianity offered 'a total escape from reality by holding out the promise of a kingdom able to overthrow all the worthless institutions which sustained society',[106] but his generalization would need more extensive support than seems to be available in the actual texts. In a Judaean context, opposition to Roman rule would be relevant, but is hard to find in the gospels. It could well be that there is in the texts an indication of hostility to the present order of things in the Temple, and the belief that the existing Temple would be purged, or destroyed, or replaced in the new age.[107] Certainly Jesus does seem to have been regarded as a threat to the existing order both by the Romans who were directly responsible for his execution, and by the Sadducees who may well have wished to see a swift end to a threat to their control of the Temple. But most of Jesus's activities seem to have taken place in and around Galilee, and this was mostly territory controlled by Herod Antipas. John the Baptist did indeed fall foul of Herod Antipas, but apparently for criticizing his second marriage. The gospels suggest criticism of Antipas by Jesus (Mark 8.15), and a threat by Antipas directed against Jesus (Luke 13.31–3).[108] Had Jesus or John advocated violent revolt, the situation would have been very different. One cannot exclude a threat to the existing order from the message of the Kingdom, but that message seems to have looked to *God* to change the existing order of things, and not to have urged overt political action. Modern attempts to distinguish religion and politics are inappropriate here. In the ancient world, and in first-century Judaism, the two were intimately connected. But though Jesus's proclamation of the Kingdom challenged the existing pattern of things, it did so by calling its values and its ultimate future into question, not by advocating the sort of military adventures envisaged in the War Scroll from Qumran. It is in this sense also, perhaps, that we should understand Jesus's attitude to property. He did not in any way lead a movement against those with possessions, though possessions and the rich are certainly sharply criticized in the gospel tradition. Not all of those who responded to Jesus abandoned their property, though Jesus and his immediate followers did so.

The particular character of Jesus's message about the Reign of God also sets it apart from other apocalyptic movements, as well as inviting comparison with them. But we cannot pursue that issue here.

To see Jesus's renunciation of possessions as coming from the challenge of the Reign of God to all existing values is to direct attention to the more negative aspect of his message. What then is the corresponding positive, and where can we find in Jesus's teaching a portrayal of the Kingdom which goes further than the parables depicting the joyful discovery of hidden treasure or of a priceless pearl? The poetic denunciation of cares may offer us an answer.

On Cares
(Luke 12.22–32; Matt. 6.25–34)
(cf. Thomas log. 36 and pap. Oxy. 4.655)

We must first ask about the different versions of the passage. Pap. Oxy. 4.655 and Thomas log. 36 seem to be of little independent value. Both are concerned with the theme of removing clothing (i.e. the human body) and becoming sons of the living one. The Greek version is closer to the Synoptics than the Coptic, which focuses exclusively on the gnostic obsession with clothing.[109] The Greek version mentions stature, and (probably) food as well as clothing.

Matthew has inserted the passage into his Sermon on the Mount, but the indications from Luke suggest that it stood elsewhere in Q. It is also widely agreed that Matthew contains an addition at the end.[110] But even the version common to Matthew and Luke is thought to have been expanded. The basic unit is probably the double comparison with the ravens and the lilies in Luke 12.24; 12.27–8. This is set out as follows by Manson:

I	Consider the ravens,	(a)
	That they neither sow nor reap;	(b_1)
	They have no barn or storehouse;	(b_2)
	And God feeds them:	(d)
	How much better are you than the birds!	(f)
II	Consider the lilies,	(a)
	How they neither toil nor spin,	(b)
	Yet I tell you that Solomon in all his glory was not arrayed like one of these.	(c)
	But if God so clothe the grass	(d)
	Which today is in the field	(e_1)
	And tomorrow is cast into the oven;	(e_2)
	How much more you, O ye of little faith?	(f)

Fuchs provides an almost identical arrangement.[111]

The additional material makes the passage more of a polemic against anxious effort to secure food and clothing.[112] Where does such a concern belong in the tradition? Fuchs speaks of the difficulties faced by the whole community in a time of persecution.[113] In favour of this might be the context in Q, since persecution is referred to in Luke 12.4–11. But one could also think of the use of this passage during the more general hardships and difficulties of the early years of the Church. Others have noted the similarity of theme between this passage and the mission charge[114] and seen here a reference to the insecurity faced by the apostles. Certainly apostles and wandering prophets were expected to abandon ordinary concerns and rely on their converts to provide food and other necessities. These suggestions may show us how the passage was understood in the early Church, but the original poem seems to envisage a more radical dependence on nature than the rules of the mission charge. All the same it seems more likely that it has some connection with the lifestyle of wandering charismatics, and is not simply a homily telling Galilean farmers to worry less about their crops. Nor do we have here the simple adoption of a piece of popular piety urging trust in providence.[115] Käsemann comments that 'the Jewish belief in Providence is modified in a very odd fashion'.[116] Indeed it is.

The Cynics certainly taught that one could depend upon nature for all one's needs, but in saying that, they also advocated the limitation of need. The man who limits his needs, and is able to enjoy the wealth of nature, is closest to the gods, who 'need nothing'. But what we have in the gospels is very different from such thoughts. Miraculous feeding by God is mentioned in the Hebrew Bible, in the manna tradition of Exodus 16, and in the story of Elijah and the ravens in 1 Kings 17. But in the synoptic passage we are discussing, it is not miraculous, but regular, provision of food which is envisaged, such as was provided for Adam in the garden of Eden. According to the myth, the need for clothes and the need to work for food came after the fall. In rabbinic Judaism we find an extremely interesting observation on the relation between work, care, and food. In the course of a brief discussion of the choice of crafts to teach one's son, the following remarks are attributed to R. Simeon b. Eleazar:

> Hast thou ever seen a wild animal or a bird practising a craft? —yet they have their sustenance without care and were they not created for naught else but to serve me? But I was created to serve my Maker. How much more then ought not I to have my sustenance without care? But I have wrought evil, and for-

feited my sustenance [i.e. forfeited my right to sustenance without care]. [Kid. 4.14, trans. Danby.]

This rabbinic utterance is in direct conflict with the teaching of the poetic denunciation of cares. The rabbi is following Genesis 3.17–19 and arguing that man sinned, and was condemned to earn his bread with toil and sweat. The saying of Jesus seems to pay no attention to this emphasis on the fall. Jesus calls for faith (Luke 12.28 par.)[117] and advocates a simple dependence upon God characteristic of paradisal conditions. But how are we to understand such an extremely radical demand for trust and freedom from care?

Perhaps some further passages about 'care' may throw some light on the matter. In 1 Corinthians 7.32 being without care is coupled with caring for the things of the Lord, and contrasted with care for the things of the world. The whole context is one in which it is argued that though marriage is permitted, to remain unmarried is preferable in view of the imminence of the coming Kingdom. In an interpretative passage in Mark 4.19, cares are designated 'cares of the age', or cares of this aeon. Perhaps these hints may provide a clue. To live without care is to live in the new age. The Reign of God brings about a new situation in which total trust is evoked, and in which a new dependence on God is expected. We may have traces of the lengths to which some early Christians took such thoughts in the strange disorders at Thessalonika (1 Thess. 4.11). Whether this was simply a case of people taking advantage of early Christian charity, or whether people were stopping work in expectation of the parousia is not wholly certain, but the latter possibility makes good sense of the texts.[118] The troubles may have been severe enough to require recourse to the old adage: 'If any one will not work, let him not eat' (2 Thess. 3.10b). Certainly the poetic denunciation of cares seems to have caused disorders much later among the monks of North Africa.[119]

The teaching on cares is in conflict with the conventional wisdom of texts such as Proverbs 6.6, with its realistic observations about the diligence of the ant. In the saying about the ravens and the lilies, we find a different appeal to nature. We cannot prove that it must be attributed to Jesus rather than to early Christian enthusiasm. But we can note that the attitude is compatible with the act of plucking ears of corn on the Sabbath (Mark 2.23–8), or the boldness of the appeal behind Moses to 'the beginning' which is made in the sayings about marriage (Mark 10.5–9) and the Sabbath. The Reign of God brings the end time, which recaptures the fabled bliss of the beginning of things. We have seen already that the Reign of God was proclaimed as bringing good news to the poor and healing to the sick and afflicted. It brings forgiveness, and an end to Satan's rule (Luke 10.18; Mark 3.26). It is described as a feast, and compared to a treasure or a pearl beyond price. But the time of the coming of the Kingdom is also a time of trust, when protection is no longer appropriate (Matt. 10.10 par; Luke 9.3; 10.3–4), and when anxious effort for food and clothing is no longer in place. Though the Reign of God is not simply seen as a return to the beginning, a paradisal element is present in this teaching about the Kingdom.

POVERTY AND THE REIGN OF GOD

Jesus expected a sudden and dramatic future intervention by God. But he also believed that the present was already a time of decision, of joy, of healing, and of new beginnings. Why did this message about the Kingdom lead Jesus and his followers *both* to expect an end to poverty *and* to adopt the role of destitute itinerants? On the one hand there was the hope of a new age which would end sickness and poverty, and bring back the lost and the rejected. On the other hand the need to proclaim the coming Reign of God led Jesus and his followers to adopt the life of wandering preachers. They travelled without resources, and without protection as witnesses to the coming Kingdom, in trust and dependence on God and on those who would feed and shelter them. The more formal pattern of wandering Christian apostles and communal charity was preceded by this simpler and more spontaneous surrender of resources and possessions. Joy rather than severity seems to have been the mark of their willing sacrifice. Like the finder of unexpected treasure or a priceless pearl, they abandoned everything for the Kingdom. In comparison with this, all other duties and values paled into insignificance. The saying about the ravens and the lilies points to a paradisal element in the teaching of Jesus. It advocates a trust and dependence on God appropriate to the fabled era of primal innocence. But such an outlook is not surprising from one who addressed God with the simple directness of *Abba*, and who asked today for the bread of the coming age.

FIVE

Conclusions and Contemporary Postscript

CONCLUSIONS

The gulf between the strata of Palestinian society in the first century of our era was by no means exclusively an economic one. This study has, however, been chiefly concerned with the economic aspects of a society which was also divided by race, descent, and religious status, as well as by wealth and poverty. Many of the pronouncements which we find in the gospels on the subject of poverty and riches reflect the gulf that existed between rich and poor in the Ancient Near East. Yet more important even than this, as a background to the sayings and narratives concerned with possessions and discipleship, were the turbulent social and economic events of the period in question. We have examined those sayings and those narratives in the light of the history of the tradition, considering in turn the redaction, the sources, the oral tradition, and the teaching and activity of Jesus. The picture which emerges from that critical study of the tradition must now be considered as a totality. The conclusions suggest that there is much to commend the view that the successive layers of the tradition reflect the changing social and economic circumstances of the period. The teaching of Jesus not only (incidentally) offers a picture of life in Galilee which is in accord with the data assembled from other sources. Central to the teaching and activity of Jesus was a passionate concern for the dawning Reign of God. The period was one of turbulence, and the movement inaugurated by Jesus was one of a number of new movements. It is to be distinguished not by its character of response to the troubles and expectations of the time, but rather by the quality and nature of its response. Second, early Christianity does seem to reflect in its teaching on possessions the economically precarious circumstances of its origins in Jerusalem, and the severe hardships of the famine. Then third, the evangelists Matthew and Luke in their turn reflect, in their redaction of the same motif, the more settled period of a time subsequent to the Jewish revolt, and perhaps also a geographical as well as a temporal distance from the earlier troubles. We must consider each of these factors in turn.

Jesus and his first disciples stand at the beginning of the story. A charismatic prophet and healer, with an apocalyptic message about the Reign of God, inevitably in certain respects invites comparison with other leaders of 'millenarian' movements. Both similarities, and also certain differences, emerge from the pursuit of such comparisons. Our concern is with only some of those features. Jesus seems to have attracted an open circle of adherents, not all of whom became close followers. The latter certainly left behind both family and possessions and led an itinerant life as associates of the one who proclaimed the new age. Yet though the break with the old life was certainly radical, it did not have the character of the exclusivism and even hatred practised by certain modern sectarians. Nor does Jesus seem to have insisted that all his hearers respond in precisely the way his closest followers did. There is not evidence of any formal 'double standard' here, merely indications that, in a relatively open circle of adherents, a variety of response was tolerated. Certainly the reports suggest that the disciples of Jesus were as varied a group as the adherents of other eschatological movements.

The stories mention fishermen, and a fisherman's sons, a tax collector, a Zealot(!), and women, one of whom was the wife of an official of Herod Antipas. The group was hardly monochrome, and if there was an inner circle of twelve, there was variety even there too. There is little evidence that the movement had either zealotic or para-zealotic tendencies. If a sociological description in this area is required, one might rather hazard the guess that the movement belonged to a situation that was 'pre-political'. Certainly we should be cautious about reading back the revolutionary character of A.D. 60–66 into the time of Herod Antipas and Pontius Pilate. But Jesus did expect a radical change in the order of things. Indeed he seems to have proclaimed that God's Reign had already taken people by surprise. But what is the character of that Reign? The images in which it is portrayed give some indication. It is characterized by feasting and by healing, it is good news for the poor, it brings an end to hunger, sickness, and oppression, an end to Satan's rule. Some of these images can be interpreted in a spiritual manner, but such an interpretation should not, as we have seen, be carried so far as to avoid the more direct reference that often seems to be required. Not only Jesus's message but also his conduct is significant. He and his closest followers left behind both family and possessions. They moved from place to place, and they depended on charity and hospitality. Their attitude of trust and dependence was carried very far, and it seems that it was their belief about the Kingdom which led to this 'utopian', or paradisal, or 'millenarian' aspect of the movement. The hearers of Jesus were urged not to worry about clothing, or food, or protection. Such cares, in Jewish perspective, came as a result of the fall, and it was after the loss of Eden that there came the need to worry about food and clothing, the necessity of earning one's bread with toil, and the war and hatred that disfigure human history. Jesus's teaching and activity assumed that a new era was already dawning. The new evaluation of possessions implicit in all this comes to the fore in Jesus's parables of the treasure and the pearl, and in the poetic denunciation of cares. Here too we find the ultimate origin of the stories about the demands required of new disciples, and of the pattern of life presupposed in the mission charge. Perhaps also to be included here are those passages which warn against the dangers of riches, and which urge generosity.

If the death of Jesus upset the immediate apocalyptic hopes of his followers, and brought an accentuated realization of the antipathy of a larger community, it was swiftly succeeded by the conviction that Jesus had been resurrected, and would soon return in power. Socially the new community which held these beliefs was tightly knit. Economically it was precarious. The apostles and the poor needed to be supported by their co-religionists, and a high level of mutual support seems to have been forthcoming. The narratives in Acts may reveal literary and rhetorical motifs, but the accounts of generous giving seem not to have been utterly distant from the reality. The pattern quickly seems to have established itself that more settled members of the community supported weaker members and itinerant charismatics. Perhaps the division between residents and itinerants was not always hard and fast. Certainly during this period, and in such circumstances, the teaching which urged generosity would have been especially valued. Thus the injunctions to lay up treasure in heaven, or to choose between God and mammon, would have seemed especially appropriate. Also, if the rich remained aloof from the new movement, it is hardly surprising that the community treasured sayings such as that about the eye of the needle, and preserved parables such as that about the rich fool. Motifs similar to those just listed are found in more than one of the sources.

During the period of the famine the problems which more generally affected this period came to a head, at least for Christians living in the area directly affected by the famine. Already early Christianity had a separate system of poor relief, and now this seems to have broken down seriously in the face of the desperate shortage of bread. It is especially in the sources used by Luke that we find passages which seem to contain the motif of resentment against the rich and well fed, allied with a theology of reversal. These motifs are especially acute in the woes and in the story of Dives and Lazarus, and perhaps also partly visible in the Magnificat.

Yet the strongest long-term trend was one of routinization. The *ad hoc* decisions of a more charismatic beginning became institutionalized, and phrases which no doubt once belonged to a situation where mendicant itinerancy was the norm, got repeated in more settled communities of believers. The repetition of teaching designed for an earlier epoch is a common enough feature of religious communities. Sometimes adaptation was necessary. This may have been the case in the passage about the sword in Luke 22.35–8. It was certainly the case when Paul interpreted the demand that apostles depend on hospitality, as a privilege he graciously surrendered in the interests of his converts.

The period of the evangelists marks the furthest limits of our present study. Mark we have largely considered with the sources, and much in Mark reflects the period of the sources. Yet though that Gospel may well reflect an era of uncertainty and persecution, there are traces that, already in the redaction of Mark, the earlier more severe teaching about possessions was being modified. The case of Luke is more interesting. Though Luke retains much which he has inherited from his sources, including some very fierce denunciations of the rich, yet his familiarity with the culture and ways of business of the more affluent poses a problem of interpretation. Luke's own redactional activity suggests that he did not accentuate the hostility to riches which reached him from his sources. The best interpretation of his editorial traits seems to be that he wished to emphasize the spiritual dangers of riches, rather than express direct hostility to the rich. Indeed his concern may well have been to warn of the dangers, rather than to utter menacing threats. It is in Matthew, however, that we have the clearest examples of the harshness of the earlier traditions being modified. Matthew is milder than Mark on the subject of property and riches, and Matthew's version of Q sayings is on several occasions milder than the version Luke seems to have inherited. Some accommodation to the values implicit in a settled community of believers who owned possessions seems to have happened throughout earliest Christianity. In Matthew we seem to have the greatest degree of that accommodation to intractable reality to be found within the gospels. Yet even Matthew has preserved passages which incorporate Jesus's presentation of the challenge to existing values by the supreme worth of the coming Reign of God. And even Matthew also records something of the hardships required of disciples and faced by them.

The conclusions we have listed indicate the importance of examining not only the teaching on wealth and poverty, but also the economic circumstances of early Christianity, and the tide of social and economic events. It is also important, though not the primary aim of this study, to bear in mind insights derived from the study of other eschatologically orientated, or 'millenarian', movements. Finally at the end of our study some brief comments on the significance of the results may not be wholly inappropriate. Biblical study sometimes leaves the impression that once the meaning of the text or texts has been established, there the task is ended. I certainly do not wish to leave any such impression. The very variety of motifs which have been uncovered, and the indications of changes of views in changing circumstances, show that the question of interpretation or application is far from simple. Undoubtedly the image of discipleship without possessions, expressed in some of the texts, has held the imagination of many, and has inspired some to the sort of heroic virtue displayed by Christians such as Francis of Assisi. It is true that such thoroughgoing imitation of the life of Jesus has more often been praised than practised, and also that the motivation of its appeal would make an interesting study in itself. But our concern is more with what appears in the New Testament than with what others have made of it.

At the heart of Jesus's teaching is his message about the Reign of God. His teaching is then concerned with an ideal, yet not with some timeless ideal, but rather with a dream or vision of what the future could and should be like. This eschatological perspective gives priority to hope and to the future, and thereby calls the present and all its values into question. Jesus was not a political revolutionary, nor was he overtly or actively much concerned with political matters. In so far as there are political and social implications of his teaching, these spring from a deeper level than direct prescriptions, and were expressed not only in his words about God's reign, but also in the defencelessness and open trust of his itinerant ministry, and in the common life of the earliest Church.

This challenge by Jesus to the values inherent in a world of possessions was subject to at least two lines of reinterpretation. The one was to turn it into an attack on wealth and its possessors as such. The motif of resentment linked to a theology of reversal is one instance of such a reinterpretation of the message. The danger is that such adaptation replaces the openness of Jesus with an exclusivist outlook governed by resentment. The opposite tendency appears when accommodation is made to the existing order of things, characterized by settled communities with an ever greater 'sufficiency' of possessions. In Matthew that tendency is becoming apparent. This also eventually comes in conflict with the original vision, not immediately, but when realism about the present leads to the loss of the dream of paradise to be restored.

CONTEMPORARY POSTSCRIPT: SOCIAL ETHICS AND THE GOSPELS

One of the most pressing contemporary problems is the great gulf between rich and poor not only within societies but also between different political states. Faced with massive evidence of severe deprivation, it is hardly surprising that older traditions have been re-examined and newer ideologies have been propounded in an attempt to remedy a desperate disorder. The wider implications of this question cannot possibly be considered here, but it is relevant to see how the evidence of the New Testament has been and might be used in this connection. I propose, therefore, to review some of the pronouncements about this question made by modern Christians and to look especially at their handling of the New Testament evidence. If I conclude that the use of this evidence is sometimes rather superficial, this is not due to any lack of agreement on my part with the urgent need to remedy those gross injustices and inequalities which should offend all civilized consciences. A good cause should not be spoiled by invalid arguments, and ineffective arguments can often be replaced by better ones.

The liberation theologians of Latin America have produced some of the most vigorous recent writing on this subject. The have challenged traditional interpretations of the Bible and attempted to read the texts afresh in the light of the exploitation and revolutionary struggles of their modern environment. Those who are instinctively alienated by such an approach would do well to consider the implications of the argument (in the preceding chapters) that, both in the ancient world and today, economic and moral opinions often reflect the prevailing social and economic situation. (This argument cuts many ways.)

Miranda argues that *differentiating ownership* can always be traced back to acts of injustice and spoliation.[1] He cites the prophets and patristic writers as expressing this view, and looks to the New Testament for further support. But here he tends to overstate his case. Naturally he cites the most extreme passages from Luke's sources, but he does not very vigorously ask about their provenance or consider how typical they are.[2] I have argued that these passages sometimes reflect the outlook of impoverished Christians during the period of the famine. They certainly expess a fierce denunciation of wealth, but they do not say that all differentiating ownership results from theft. Miranda also cites Mark 10.25 as against such ownership. The passage certainly says that salvation is virtually impossible for the rich, and in the accompanying tale a rich man is asked to surrender all his possessions, but the gospels do not condemn ownership altogether. Nor does a single reference to 'unrighteous mammon' in Luke 16.9 mean that all possessions are ill-gotten. In Matt. 6.1–2, and in the Hebrew Bible, alms are spoken of as 'righteousness' ('justice'). But this does not prove that alms were seen as the restoration of what had been stolen from the poor.[3] The prophets denounced injustice to, and oppression of, the poor, and the laws tried to remedy matters. This is presumably the background to the designation of alms as 'righteousness'. It does seem that Miranda has overstated his case, though some of what he says draws attention to important features of the texts.

Guttierez at one point makes a great deal of claims that Jesus associated with Zealots and of the evidence that he was condemned on a political charge. Yet Guttierez admits, as almost all serious students of the gospels do, that Jesus was not a Zealot.[4] Guttierez is on better ground when drawing attention to political implications of Jesus's teaching about the coming Reign of God. He rightly notes that the Hebrew prophets and the Pentateuchal laws refused to tolerate extremes of poverty and riches. He is rather selective in his treatment of the New Testament, and in his final chapter he concentrates mainly on the Lucan version of the beatitudes.[5] Though he focuses on this one passage he does correctly say that this version beatifies the materially poor. He also connects this with the beginning of the Kingdom of God when the blind are given sight and the hungry fed, and the elimination of exploitation has begun.

The borderland between social ethics and biblical study is also explored in various more official documents and pronouncements. The document *Gaudium et Spes* from the Second Vatican Council has sections on social justice and on ownership (29.71–2). These largely appeal to general ethical principles and to earlier encyclicals. They thereby wisely avoid some of the difficulties inherent in the attempt to base a modern social ethic directly on the New Testament. But passages from the gospels are cited (e.g. Luke 3.11; 10.30ff.; 11.41; Mark 8.36; 12.39–41 in section 72; and Luke 16.19–31 and Matt. 25.40 in section 27), though mostly without further comment. Other documents such as *Lumen Gentium* 8 refer to the poverty of Christ (citing 2 Cor. 8.9) and his mission 'to bring good news to the poor' (Luke 4.18). The 1967 papal encyclical *Populorum Progressio* deals with the subject at greater length and cites several passages from the gospels and epistles.[6] Inevitably in documents of this nature the biblical references are sparing, briefly made, and not always indicative of the full range and complexity of the texts in question. One needs to turn to more extended studies by Roman Catholic biblical scholars for more detailed discussion.[7]

Recent pronouncements from the World Council of Churches leave no doubt about the level of attention given by that body to the acute poverty that is all too widespread in the modern world. But though the official reports from Uppsala (1968) and Nairobi (1975) both offer some theological grounds for a great deal of exhortation on this subject, they provide very little detailed ethical or biblical backing. The Nairobi report talks of Christ being born into poverty, and of following Christ 'on the same path committed to the cause of the poor, oppressed, and rejected'.[8] But these statements are vague, ambiguous, and insufficiently supported. It is not clear that being 'committed to the cause of the poor' means the same thing in the context of the report and in the context of the life of Jesus. The same report also bases the call for a just society on the command to love one's neighbour, but the point is not developed in detail.[9] There are, of course, difficulties about finding a biblical basis for social ethics, but if more attention had been paid to this question it might have narrowed the gulf between the WCC and some of its critics. One does, of course, need to remember that earlier reports from the Ecumenical Movement did devote more attention to the basis of social ethics, and that separate documents from related sources do consider the question. Thus Charles Elliott discusses the relation between love and justice in the teaching of the gospels, and emphasizes that love includes the claims of justice as well as going beyond them. He notes the importance of the Hebrew prophets, and also draws attention to the relevance for social ethics of New Testament eschatology. There the present order is seen as in need of recreation and transformation.[10]

In contrast to official reports some more popular works cite a very considerable number of biblical texts but in a rather indiscriminate manner, and with a tendency to proceed directly from isolated texts to injunctions directed at the modern world. One can hardly complain here that the relevant texts have not been assembled. But one can ask whether sufficient attention has been paid either to the original contexts and the meaning of those texts, or to the distance that separates the ancient world from ours.[11] Even more alarming are activities of some fringe religious sects. Where their leaders and their members alike practise renunciation of material goods, one may feel that a particular feature of early Christianity has been turned into an imposed ideal. But if it is the members who are ordered to practise poverty while the leaders benefit substantially from their sacrifices, then this situation would seem to be very far from that of early Christianity.

Faced with the difficulty of relating modern social ethics and biblical teaching some writers have opted for more radical solutions. In the 1978 Reith Lectures the Revd Dr Edward Norman uttered some severe but not wholly unjustified criticisms of the 'conflation of Christian love of neighbour with the most hardline

Marxist devices to engineer radical social change'.[12] He insists that religion is essentially concerned with 'the ethereal qualities of immortality'. But when he gives the impression that Jesus was only concerned with personal morality and religion, he is in conflict with the evidence of the gospels, as can readily be seen from the preceding sections of this book. Indeed Norman's own brief excursion into a description of the activity of Jesus shows an astounding naivety about the gospels.[13] Norman does indeed admit at one point that the teaching of Jesus has social implications, but he seems as reluctant to admit this as Guttierez was to admit that Jesus was not a Zealot.

The Graeco-Roman historian de Ste Croix also holds that the New Testament places little emphasis on social ethics. He, however, reaches a conclusion diametrically opposed to that of Dr Norman. He severely criticizes early Christianity for placing its emphasis on almsgiving rather than on programmes of social justice.[14] He considers a brief selection of passages from the gospels and also the teaching of the patristic writers. Now it is good to have a fresh voice interrogating the rather cloistered world of New Testament scholarship, and it would be unfair to complain about minor details rather than discuss his main point. Certainly it is true that the Hebrew prophets do provide a clearer and more definite social ethic than early Christianity, and this fact needs to be acknowledged. It is also true that Christianity after Constantine could have moved further in the desired direction than it did. But in the New Testament period Christians were in no position to engage in national or international social and economic reform. To criticize them on that score is to overlook such relevant teaching as does exist, and to indulge in the quaint anachronism of those who criticize the Hittites for not inventing railways, or who remonstrate with Aristotle for not employing predicate calculus. The gospels do not advocate an economic programme, but they do call for a love which both includes and exceeds the demands of justice. The issue is an important one for Christians and for others, as de Ste Croix says, for the figure of Jesus is a powerful symbol even for those who do not subscribe to some of the more highly developed Christian doctrines.

What then are the conclusions to be drawn from this final section? It is true that the New Testament is more obviously concerned with belief and with the ethics of life in small communities rather than with broader political issues. It is also true that the gospels do not elaborate a social ethic, and even if they had it would have reflected the social circumstances of the first century, and been only indirectly applicable to the complex modern industrial world. But it is not true that a concern with social ethics is wholly absent from, or alien to, the gospels. And it is certainly not true that either Jesus or his immediate disciples simply endorsed the existing order in general or the gulf between rich and poor in particular. Rather, they saw the sufferings of the poor as part of the evil of the present order which was in need of being transformed. Nor did Jesus see the coming Reign of God as something wholly separate from his own actions. He believed that in his healing activity the future Reign of God was already transforming the present. Jesus and his disciples led no political revolt, but they did sharply criticize accumulation of wealth and neglect of the poor. Some of the sources go further than others in this respect, but both the Hebrew Bible and the New Testament are highly critical of any state of affairs in which some have plenty while others starve. It may not be a simple matter to found a modern social and political theory directly on the gospels, but the New Testament gives no comfort to those who think that religion or morality can turn a blind eye to oppression, injustice, or flagrant inequalities. The teaching of Jesus and of the gospels is rather to call people to participate now in a new order in which love both includes and exceeds the demands of justice.

But if the claim that God and his demands are just is to be more than a tautology, it means that the ethical contribution to theistic language is one of the most fundamental, and that the question of the nature of justice cannot be evaded. To draw attention to the social and ethical dimensions of New Testament teaching is not to say how precisely in specified contexts love and justice are to resolve the different, and sometimes conflicting, claims of rights, deserts, and needs.[15] A number of different political alternatives are available at this point.[16] How, in detail, the demands of social justice are best met in a complex modern international economy is the kind of major and important question which must be pursued elsewhere than in this more restricted study whose original limits have already been exceeded.

Appendix A

Studies on Property and Riches in the New Testament

A more extensive range of literature is listed here than can conveniently be placed in a footnote.

Bammel, E., '*Ptōchos*' in *TDNT*, 6, pp. 885, 888–915.

Batey, R., *Jesus and the Poor*. New York, Harper, 1972.

Bornhäuser, K., *Der Christ und seine Habe nach dem N.T.* (BFCT). Gütersloh, Bertelsmann, 1936.

Braun, H., *Spätjüdisch-häretischer und frühchristlicher Radikalismus*, II (BHT) (Tübingen, Mohr, 1957), pp. 73–80.

Campenhausen, H. von, 'Early Christian Asceticism' (German edn 1949) in *Tradition and Life in the Church* (Eng. trans. Collins 1968), pp. 90–122.

Degenhardt, H. J., *Lukas, Evangelist der Armen*. Stuttgart, Kath. Bibelwerk, 1965.

Dupont, J., *Les Béatitudes*, I, Louvain, Nauwelaerts, 1958; III, Paris, Gabalda, 1973.

Greeven, H., *Das Hauptproblem der Sozialethik in der neueren Stoa und im Urchristentum* (Gütersloh, Bertelsmann, 1935), pp. 93ff.

Hauck, F., *Die Stellung des Urchristentums zu Arbeit und Geld* (BFCT). Gütersloh, Bertelsmann, 1921.

Hengel, M., *Nachfolge und Charisma* (BZNW 34), Berlin, Töpelmann, 1968.

Hengel, M., *Property and Riches in the Early Church*. SCM Press, 1974.

Kautsky, K., *The Foundations of Christianity*. German edn 1908. Eng. trans. Allen & Unwin 1925.

Kretschmar, G., 'Ein Beitrag zur Frage nach dem Ursprung frühchristlicher Askese', in *ZTK*, 61 (1964), pp. 27–67.

Légasse, S., *L'Appel du riche* (V. S. Coll. Annexe I), Paris, Beauchesne, 1966.

Leipoldt, J., *Der soziale Gedanke in der altchristlichen Kirche*. Leipzig, Koehler & Amelang, 1952.

Lohmeyer, E., *Soziale Fragen im Urchristentum* (Wissenschaft und Bildung). Leipzig, Quelle & Meyer, 1921.

Percy, E., *Die Botschaft Jesu* (LUA) (Lund, Gleerup, 1953), pp. 40–108, 168–74.

Pöhlmann, R. von, *Geschichte der sozialen Frage und des Sozialismus in der antiken Welt* (Munich, Beck, [3]1925), pp. 464ff..

Rauschenbusch, W., *Christianity and the Social Crisis*. New York, Macmillan, 1907.

Rogge, C., *Der irdische Besitz im Neuen Testament*. Göttingen, Vandenhoeck u. Ruprecht, 1897.

Schnackenburg, R., *The Moral Teaching of the New Testament* (G. 1962) (Freiburg and London, Herder, 1965), §13, pp. 121–132.

Scott, E. F., *The Ethical Teaching of Jesus* (New York, Macmillan, 1925), pp. 51ff., 89ff.

Shailer Mathews, A. M., *The Social Teaching of Jesus*. New York and London, Macmillan, 1897.

Ste Croix, G. E. M. de, 'Early Christian Attitudes to Property and Slavery' in *Church, Society, and Politics* ed. D. Baker (*Studies in Church History* 12) (Blackwell 1975), pp. 1–38.

Steinmann, A., *Jesus und die soziale Frage*. Paderborn, Schöningh, [2]1925.

Theissen, G., *The First Followers of Jesus: A Sociological Analysis of the Earliest Christianity* (London, SCM, 1978) (= Soziologie der Jesusbewegung).

Troeltsch, E., *The Social Teaching of the Christian Churches*. German edn 1911. Eng. trans. Allen & Unwin 1931.

Vökl, R., *Christ und Welt nach dem Neuen Testament* (Würzburg, Echter, 1961), pp. 20ff.

My manuscript was prepared for publication before the appearance of the useful work by L. Schottroff and W. Stegemann, *Jesus von Nazareth – Hoffnung der Armen*. Stuttgart, Kohlhammer, 1978.

Appendix B

On 'ānî and 'ānāw

The prophets of the Hebrew Bible criticized the rich who oppressed and crushed the poor. In the laws there are various safeguards aimed at protecting the poor. In the psalms can be found the hope of 'the poor' that God will restore the fortunes of those unjustly oppressed. Much attention has been paid to these passages.[1] Some have identified the speakers as a social group within the nation. Others have argued that the emphasis on the righteousness and innocence of 'the poor' means that the term referred mainly to a pious group. But others again have pointed out that in some cases at least the psalms utter the sentiments of the whole nation oppressed by a hostile foreign power. There are a number of issues here not all of which can be pursued in detail in the present work. It does seem to be the case that some at least of the utterances of 'the poor' reflect the plight of the whole nation. This does not exclude the possibility that such utterances could also be made by groups within the nation, and this certainly seems to have happened in texts produced after the close of the Hebrew canon. Further, the fact that 'the poor' plead the righteousness or innocence of their cause does not mean that the term 'poor' can *simply* be regarded as an equivalent for 'pious'. The primary reference is usually to suffering, although that suffering may almost always in such texts be presented as the undeserved suffering of the righteous who look to God for recompense.

The specific terms *'ānî* and *'ānāw* present an additional problem. It is not clear how far these words are to be distinguished from each other.[2] Quite apart from their general similarity, there is sometimes variation between *K^e^tî̱ḇ* and *Q^e^rê*. In later Hebrew, *'ānî* refers to the poor, and *'ānāw* to the meek.[3] Attempts may have been made to press the later distinction in earlier texts.

The normal meaning of *'ānî* is 'humbled', 'oppressed', and so 'poor'.[4] Because the oppressed poor appeal to God for justice, they regard themselves as righteous, in that they have been wronged, and are in the right in pressing their case.[5] In context the antonyms for *'ānî* are often words meaning 'violent',[6] which indicates that *'ānî* means 'oppressed'.

'ānāw means 'poor', 'humble', or 'meek'.[7] But does it refer to a humble attitude or humble status? The translators of the LXX rendered the word variously,[8] but with a slight preference for 'humble' or 'meek'. This suggests that it shares the ambiguity of the English word 'humble'. The context is often a more reliable guide. In the Hebrew Bible the word is used of the poor and needy who seek the Lord.[9] They are also contrasted with the wicked and arrogant.[10] The *'anāwîm* are therefore the humble and meek, i.e. those who patiently endure their reduced status, and look to God for justice. This perhaps implies righteousness, but in the sense that they have a just claim. There may be a difference between *'ānî* and *'ānāw*, but it should not be exaggerated.

So *'ānî* refers to the oppressed poor, and *'ānāw* to the humble and meek. But the former possess a sense of righteousness; and the genuinely humble status of the latter needs to be recognized.

In the Hebrew Bible poverty is seen as a ground for compassion and generosity; it is also a reason for well-justified claims for redress. The poor see themselves as wronged, as in the right in pressing their cause, and they humbly plead with their God. But in the Hebrew Bible poverty is not a religious ideal, it is not sought as a virtue. Subsequent writings, such as the Psalms of Solomon, take up the motif which we have noted in the canonical psalms. These psalms also plead before God the cause of the poor who are in distress, but deserve deliverance (Ps. Sol. 5.2, 11; 15.2; 18.2). Though the poor in question are also seen as pious (Ps. Sol. 10.6) there is no doubt that people in real distress are so designated.

The text which comes nearest to seeing an act of renunciation and temporary self-impoverishment as a ground for mercy is Joseph and Asenath 10.13—12.7. Here conversion to monotheism and ostentatious repentance are described. But Asenath has plenty of fine robes and jewels to wear later (18.3ff.).

The Qumran community on the other hand was poor, and the victim of plunder at the hands of the Wicked Priest. The Qumran texts echo the canonical psalms in using various Hebrew words to describe the community as 'poor' (1Q Hod. 2.32–5; 3.25; 5.13ff.; 1Qp Hab. 12.5–6; 12.10, cf. 12.2–6) and as 'the poor' (4Qp Ps. 37.21–2). Similar expressions are found in the War Scroll (1Q Mil. 11.13; 13.14; 14.6–7).[11]

Appendix C

Studies of the Lucan attitude to wealth

C. Campbell, *Critical Studies in St Luke's Gospel* (Edinburgh, Blackwood, 1891), pp. 171–308 makes the most of Luke's severity in comparison with Matthew and Mark. A. Plummer, *A Critical and Exegetical Commentary on the Gospel according to St Luke* (I.C.C.) (Edinburgh, Clark, 1896), pp. xxv–xxvi argues that there is no Ebionism even in Luke's source, that Luke is no more severe than Mark and is not hostile to the rich but concerned to make them less worldly. F. Hauck, *Arbeit und Geld*, pp. 81–3 argues that the sharper hostility to wealth found in Luke is due to the poverty of the Palestinian Church reflected in Luke's source. B. S. Easton, *The Gospel according to St Luke* (Edinburgh, Clark, 1926), pp. xxvii, 85, also regards the special Lucan source material as reflecting the outlook of Judaean Christians subjected to economic oppression. M. Goguel, *Introduction au Nouveau Testament* (Paris, Leroux, 1922–6), I, pp. 502–4 argued that neither Luke nor his source displayed a consistently Ebionite tendency. H. J. Cadbury, *The Making of Luke–Acts* (SPCK [2]1958), pp. 260–63 thinks Luke intensified Jesus's teaching because of the influence of the tradition, and that he urged the rich to help the poor. Greeven, *Hauptproblem der Sozialethik*, pp. 78–92 carefully examined Luke's editing of Mark and Q and argued that though Luke's teaching comes mainly from his sources he does sharpen and generalize it. H. von Campenhausen, 'Early Christian Asceticism', p. 98 thinks that Luke followed the tradition of Palestinian groups in emphasizing poverty and almsgiving but also made these ideas his own. Percy, *Botschaft*, p. 106 held, however, that the so-called Ebionism of Luke went back to Jesus. R. Koch, 'Die Wertung des Besitzes im Lukasevangelium' in *Biblica*, 38 (1957), pp. 151–9 thinks that Luke wrote for poor Christians in Graeco-Roman cities and stresses the religious dangers of riches. Conzelmann, *Theology of St Luke* (Faber 1960), p. 233 argues that the 'Ebionism' of Luke is due to the source. Dupont, *Les Béatitudes* [2]I, pp. 299–342, and III, p. 206 regards Luke as sympathetic to the poor and probably responsible for the woes, and stressing the spiritual dangers of riches. Bammel, *TDNT*, 6, p. 907 finds a concern for the salvation of the rich superimposed on passages which contain criticism of riches. Schnackenburg, *Moral Teaching*, pp. 125–32 notes Luke's emphasis on poverty but sees behind it early Christian Ebionism and the teaching of Jesus. McCormick, 'Economic Background of Luke' (see ch. 2, n. 21), notes Luke's familiarity with commerce and holds that he urges the rich to use their wealth to help others. Degenhardt, *Lukas*, esp. pp. 214–22, thinks Luke wished to teach Gentile Christians to give alms, and their church officers to avoid greed, and practise renunciation. J. Y. Thériault, 'Les dimensions sociales, économiques, et politiques dans l'oeuvre de Luc', in *Science et Esprit*, 26 (1974), pp. 205–31 notes the concern for the poor in Luke. Karris argues that Luke's church had rich and poor members and that Luke is especially concerned about the rich: cf. R. J. Karris, 'The Lukan Sitz im Leben', in *SBL 1976 Seminar Papers*, ed. G. MacRae (Missoula, Scholars Press, 1976), pp. 219–33, esp. p. 228.

Appendix D

Passages in the gospels implying the continued possession of property

It is clear from the argument of the preceding chapters that some of Jesus's disciples practised a very high degree of renunciation of property for at least some of the time. This seems to have been true of those who accompanied him during his ministry. It was also true of early Christian itinerant preachers. It is equally clear that not all of Jesus's hearers followed this example, and that many if not most of the members of the early Church lived at home and either earned or lived within their means. Many of these were expected to contribute, and no doubt did contribute generously to the movement, and it is this historical reality which gave rise to the utopian descriptions in Acts.

There are passages which commend the giving of alms or lending without expecting return (Matt. 6.3–4; Luke 6.34–5). It is hard to imagine that such passages should always be understood to be directed to sympathetic outsiders rather than to members of the new movement. Then there is the question of houses. Members of the early Church gave hospitality to those of their number who needed it, and this is no doubt the reality behind the extravagant remark about receiving in this age one hundredfold for the houses and family that disciples had surrendered (Mark 10.30). They were not all homeless itinerants, and for the mention of houses see Acts 2.46; 12.12. The sale and donation of property was not compulsory (Acts 5.4). Early Christian apocalyptic assumed that some at least of its readers lived in houses (Mark 13.15). We cannot always press details such as those given, but the picture they offer is far from implausible. Other references are more problematical. The difficulties over the house mentioned in Mark 2.15 are discussed in Chapter 4, and mean that the passage cannot be used as solid evidence in this connection. The supposition that Peter left his wife and mother-in-law (Mark 1.29–39) at home is plausible but rests on an argument from silence. The house of Martha and Mary is a favourite topic for historical romance (Luke 10.38–42; John 11.20; 12.1–2, cf. H. Bückers, *Die Biblische Lehre vom Eigentum* (Bonn, Borromäus, 1947), p. 51). But Luke does not show Jesus as eager for lavish hospitality, and the normally cautious Hauck must have been carried away when he described the house as *wohlhabend* (*Arbeit und Geld*, p. 91).

It is sometimes argued that Jesus was a friend and guest of the rich (von Campenhausen, 'Asceticism', p. 95; Schnackenburg, *Moral Teaching*, p. 125). Certainly Jesus accepted hospitality, but the evidence needs sifting. The accusation that he was a 'glutton and a drinker' (Matt. 11.19 par.) may simply reflect Deuteronomy 21.20, and in any case does not mention rich hosts. In Mark those who might seem rich associates of Jesus are few, and usually characterized by some need. Levi is a minor tax official and a social outcast; Simon a leper; and Jairus a man whose daughter has just died (Mark 2.14–15; 14.3; 5.22). Joseph of Arimathea is a man of high standing (Mark 15.43) whom Matthew calls rich (Matt. 27.57). He is the one clear instance of a rich sympathizer in Mark. Luke does like to show Jesus as guest and friend of the influential. He is invited by a *ruler* of the Pharisees (Luke 14.1). Zacchaeus is a *chief* tax collector and rich (Luke 19.2) though Luke hardly can have thought that he remained so (19.8). It is also Luke who says that the women who gave assistance to Jesus (Mark 15.40–41) included the wife of Chuza, the steward of Herod Antipas (Luke 8.1–3). There may be reminiscence in these passages, and it is not implausible that a poor itinerant preacher of a new age should accept gifts and hospitality. Plenty of parallels exist from other movements. But one also needs to remember that Luke's tendency to portray his heroes moving among the influential has not passed unnoticed. His treatment of Paul in the closing chapters of Acts is especially notable in this connection.

Notes

CHAPTER ONE
The Problem and the Economic Background to the Gospels

1 F. M. Heichelheim, 'Roman Syria', in *An Economic Survey of Ancient Rome*, ed. Tenney Frank (Baltimore, Johns Hopkins, 1938), pp. 123–254, esp. pp. 127–8.

2 On the corn yield see Ket., 112a; other details in S. W. Baron, *A Social and Religious History of the Jews* (New York, Columbia University Press, [2]1952), pp. 251–5.

3 Jos. B. J., 3.42–3 and 516–21; see also H. W. Hoehner, *Herod Antipas* (Cambridge University Press 1972), pp. 65–8. Josephus may have indulged in exaggeration. On overpopulation and the extent of the cultivation of the land see G. Theissen, *The First Followers of Jesus* (SCM Press 1978), pp. 40–46 (= Soziologie, p. 42).

4 Heichelheim, art. cit., pp. 189–208.

5 Detailed surveys of industry and commerce in Jerusalem in J. Jeremias, *Jerusalem in the Time of Jesus* (SCM Press 1969), pp. 4–57.

6 Hoehner, *Antipas*, pp. 67–9.

7 B. J., 3.414–17.

8 Heichelheim, art. cit., pp. 167–70.

9 S. Safrai and M. Stern *et al.*, *The Jewish People in the First Century* (Assen, Van Gorcum, 1974), p. 320. The sestertius was equal to one quarter of a denarius. On the titles 'prefect' and 'procurator' see E. Schürer, *The History of the Jewish People in the Age of Jesus Christ*, revised and edited by G. Vermes and F. Millar (Edinburgh, Clark, 1973), I, p. 358.

10 Jos. Ant., 19.352.

11 J. Jeremias, *Jerusalem in the Time of Jesus*, pp. 98–9.

12 Jeremias, op. cit., p. 228. See also M. Hengel, 'Das Gleichnis von den Weingärtnern Mc. 12.1–12 im Lichte der Zenonpapyri und der rabbinischen Gleichnisse' in *ZNW*, 59 (1968), pp. 1–39, esp. p. 21 on Gezer; Theissen, *The First Followers of Jesus*, p. 41 (= Soziologie, p. 42).

13 H. Kreissig, *Die Sozialen Zusammenhänge der jüdischen Krieges* (SGKA) (Berlin, Akad. V., 1970), p. 83. But see the criticisms in G. S. Gibson, 'The Social Stratification of Jewish Palestine in the First Century of the Christian Era' (unpublished dissertation, University College, London, 1975), pp. 268, 345.

14 Jeremias, op. cit., p. 303–12.

15 Kid. 22a declares that he who acquires a Jewish slave acquires a master. On the whole question see E. E. Urbach, 'The Laws Regarding Slavery as a Source for the Social History of the Period of the Second Temple, the Mishnah, and the Talmud' in *Papers of the Institute of Jewish Studies, London*, vol. I, ed. J. G. Weiss (Jerusalem, Magnes Press, 1964), pp. 1–94, esp. p. 49.

16 Jos. Vita, 71–3; Hoehner, *Antipas*, pp. 70–71. Hoehner names names, but not all of the passages to which he refers actually mention estates in Galilee. Herod the Great acquired estates by extortionate means (Jos. Ant., 17.307); see Theissen, *The First Followers of Jesus*, p. 41 (= Soziologie, p. 42). See also M. Rostovtzeff, *The Social and Economic History of the Roman Empire* (Oxford University Press [2]1957), I, p. 270, II, p. 664.

17 Jos. Vita, 33, 422.

18 Jos. B. J., 2.585.

19 For Beth Anath see P. Lond. 1948 = inv. 2661; for the rabbinic parable see Midr. Tanh. Lev. Ked. (6) 38a (Buber, p. 75); there is discussion of both texts in Hengel, 'Das Gleichnis von den Weingärtnern', 12, p. 23. See also M. Hengel, *Judaism and Hellenism* (SCM Press 1974), pp. 39–40.

20 F. C. Grant, *The Economic Background of the Gospels* (Oxford University Press 1926), p. 64.

21 Pes. 178b, Lev. R. 30.1, Ex. R. 47.5.

22 Heichelheim, art. cit., p. 163; see also V. Corbo, *The House of St Peter at Capharnaum* (Stud. Bibl. Franc., Coll. Minor 5) (Jerusalem, Franciscans, 1969).

23 For the figures see the calculations in Jeremias, op. cit., pp. 122–3.

24 Heichelheim, art. cit., p. 180. On the complexity of the question of the cost of living see D. Sperber, 'Costs of Living in Roman Palestine', in *JESHO*, 8 (1965), pp. 248–71; 9 (1966), pp. 182–211; 11 (1968), pp. 233–74; 13 (1970), pp. 1–15.

25 Some evidence of undernourishment in Palestine in the vicinity of Jerusalem is provided by N. Haas, 'Anthropological Observations on the Skeletal Remains from Giv'at ha-Mivtar', in *IEJ*, 20 (1970), pp. 38–59, esp. p. 54.

26 F. H. Heichelheim, *An Ancient Economic History*, III (Leyden, Sijthoff, 1970), p. 211.

27 Hoehner thinks it probable; see Hoehner, *Antipas*, pp. 73–5; 298–300.

28 F. C. Grant, op. cit., pp. 104–5, cf. 87ff.

29 Tac. Ann. 2.42, cf. Schürer, *History* (1973), p. 373.

30 See ch. 3, n. 2 and ch. 4, n. 54 below.

31 Jos. Ant. 19.352, cf. A. Momigliano, 'The Roman Government of Palestine', in *CAH*, 10 (Cambridge 1934), p. 851.

32 See K. F. Nickle, *The Collection* (SCM Press 1966), p. 31 following J. Jeremias, 'Sabbathjahr und N. T. Chronologie', in *ZNW*, 27 (1928). On the date see also E. Schürer, op. cit. (1973), p. 457, n. 8.

33 Jos. Ant. 20.51, cf. B.B. 11a, J. Pea 1.1.15b (53), T. Pea 4.18 (24), Pesik. R. 25 (126b); see ch. 3 below and ch. 4, n. 52.

34 Jeremias, op. cit., pp. 122–3.

35 On the date of the meeting in Jerusalem see W. G. Kümmel, *Introduction to the New Testament* (SCM Press rev. edn 1975), pp. 252–5, 294–304; and Nickle, *The Collection*, pp. 51–9. Objections to one of

the main alternatives are listed in my review of F. F. Bruce's *New Testament History* in *JTS*, 21 (1970), p. 468.

36 Schürer, op. cit., pp. 462–5.

37 Schürer, op. cit., p. 465; E. M. Smallwood, *The Jews under Roman Rule* (Leiden, Brill, 1976), p. 281.

38 On Albinus see *CAH*, 10.855 (Momigliano); Smallwood, op. cit., p. 282; and Schürer, op. cit., pp. 468–70.

39 Jos. Ant. 20.219 says over 18,000, but see Jeremias, op. cit., p. 22.

40 *CAH*, 10.853 n. (Momigliano); cf. F. F. Bruce, *New Testament History* (Nelson 1969), p. 329.

41 *CAH*, 10.855 (Momigliano).

42 See Heichelheim, 'Roman Syria', p. 182, who cites Ta'an 19b.

CHAPTER TWO
The Evangelists and their Sources

1 For a survey of the secondary literature see Appendix A, where full titles are listed. Among the more significant works are F. Hauck, *Die Stellung des Urchristentums zu Arbeit und Geld*, a detailed study of the NT texts in the light of the Jewish and Graeco-Roman background; E. Percy, *Die Botschaft Jesu*, pp. 40–108, 168–74 discusses poverty and renunciation in the gospels in the light of the Jewish background; H. Braun, *Spätjüdisch-häretischer und frühchristlicher Radikalismus*, vol. 2, pp. 73–80, is useful for its comparisons with the Qumran texts; J. Dupont, *Les Béatitudes*, I and III, discusses the attitudes of the evangelists to riches, as well as the beatitudes and woes; E. Bammel, art. '*Ptōchos*', in *TDNT*, 6, pp. 885, 888–915 is a valuable survey of the NT and other evidence; H. J. Degenhardt, *Lukas, Evangelist der Armen*, is chiefly a redactional study of Luke; S. Légasse, *L'Appel du riche*, is a detailed study of Mark 10.17–30 par.; M. Hengel, *Nachfolge und Charisma*, is valuable for discussion of the charismatic and prophetic element in stories about the call of disciples; M. Hengel, *Property and Riches in the Early Church* surveys the Jewish and Greek background, and early Christian teaching to the time of Cyprian.

2 G. D. Kilpatrick, *The Origins of the Gospel according to St Matthew*, (Oxford, Clarendon Press, 1950), pp. 125–6 notes that the money values in Matthew are higher than those in Mark and Luke. Useful insights may also be gleaned from M. D. Goulder, *Midrash and Lection in Matthew* (SPCK 1974), pp. 61–2, 109–11, even by those who dissent from the case he is arguing.

3 With L. E. Keck, 'The Poor among the Saints in the NT', in *ZNW*, 56 (1965), p. 115 and others, against Braun, *Radikalismus*, II, p. 76, n. 1. See also P. Bonnard, *L'Evangile selon S. Matthieu* (Neuchâtel, Delachaux et Niestlé, ²1970), p. 447.

4 See Bornhäuser, *Der Christ und seine Habe nach dem NT* (BFCT 38) (Gütersloh, Bertelsmann, 1936), p. 42; Bammel, *TDNT*, 6, p. 903 and n. 163. Why else should Matthew have changed it?

5 See especially the magisterial study: Dupont, *Béatitudes* III, pp. 385–471; also J. Dupont, 'Introduction aux Béatitudes', in *Nouvelle Revue*

Théologique, 98 (1976), pp. 97–108; R. A. Guelich, 'The Matthean Beatitudes: Entrance-Requirements or Eschatological Blessings?', in *JBL*, 95 (1976), pp. 415–34.

6 On *'ānî* and *'ānāw* see Appendix B. One may generally conclude that *'ānî* refers to the oppressed poor, and *'ānāw* to the humble and meek. But the former possess a sense of righteousness, and the actual humble *status* of the latter also needs to be recognized. In IQ Mil. 14.7 the *'ān^{e}wê rûaḥ* are contrasted with the 'hard of heart'; the context here and in Matthew favours the translation 'humble in spirit'. See Dupont, op. cit., pp. 389–90, 396, 427, 460–63 against a whole series of less plausible suggestions ('the fainthearted', 'the poor endowed with the Holy Spirit', 'those who are voluntarily poor').

7 On the Lucan redaction see below. The simple *ptōchoi* of Luke 6.20 preserves a version which antedates Matthew's 'poor in spirit'. In Luke's source this version, itself recalling 'the poor' of the Hebrew Bible, was understood as referring to literal poverty. Matthew presumably noted the allusion to the *^{a}nāwîm* of Isaiah 61.1 when editing the common source. On this see J. Jeremias, *New Testament Theology* I, (SCM Press 1971), pp. 112–13, though his reference to *consciousness* of spiritual poverty is an over-interpretation. See Dupont, op. cit., pp. 449–50.

8 If Matthew either dropped or did not possess the woes, and amended the blessing on the hungry, this left him free to reinterpret the blessing on the poor. He had available the whole range of meanings for *'ānî*, 'poor' and *'ānāw*, 'humble'. He seems to have preferred the connotations of the latter. In favour of the translation 'humble in spirit' are the way Matthew has edited the whole context and especially the reference to the meek (*praeis*) in 5.5. The addition of 'in spirit', and the resulting similarity to the phrase now discovered at Qumran, provide supporting evidence for the translation 'humble in spirit'. Matthew has given the beatitudes a moralizing and spiritualizing interpretation by his editing. On the whole question see Dupont, op. cit., pp. 385–471; also H. J. Degenhardt, *Lukas*, pp. 46–50.

9 Bammel, *TDNT*, 6, p. 904, with good reason.

10 The most recent monograph is that of H. J. Degenhardt, *Lukas Evangelist der Armen* (1965). A list of books and articles in Appendix C covers the period from 1891 to the present. (Authors include Campbell, Plummer, Hauck, Easton, Goguel, Cadbury, Greeven, von Campenhausen, Percy, Koch, Conzelmann, Dupont, Bammel, Schnackenburg, McCormick, Degenhardt, Thériault, Karris.)

11 Campbell emphasized Luke's severity, Hauck and Easton that of Luke's special source. Others attribute the apparent severity in varying measure to the source and to Luke (Cadbury, Greeven, von Campenhausen, Schnackenburg), while Percy attributed Luke's so-called Ebionism to Jesus. Plummer, Goguel, and McCormick minimize Luke's hostility to riches, while Koch and Dupont emphasize that Luke taught the *spiritual* danger of riches. Further details in Appendix C.

12 Luke 5.28; 8.14; 9.3; 9.25; 18.22–30; 21.4.

13 Luke 18.28, *ta idia*; cf. Mark 10.28, *panta*.

14 Luke 9.3 no staff, Luke 10.4 no sandals; compare Matt. 10.10 and contrast Mark 6.8–9.

15 Degenhardt, op. cit., pp. 51–3 argued that the vocabulary of the woes is not particularly characteristic of the Lucan redaction. H. Schürmann, *Das Lukasevangelium* (HTKNT) (Freiburg, Herder, 1969), pp. 339–41 gives arguments for regarding them as pre-Lucan (few traces of Lucan redaction, unLucan wording, similarity to James 4.9, 5.1, similarity of wording with Matthew's beatitudes suggesting omission by Matthew). But see Dupont, *Béatitudes*, I, pp. 299–342, III, pp. 205–6 for a different view. E. Schweizer, *The Good News according to Matthew* (SPCK 1976), pp. 82–3 also discusses various possibilities.

16 Schulz follows Haenchen and Strecker in holding that the divergence is not due to mistranslation. He thinks both variants redactional; cf. S. Schulz, *Q, Die Spruchquelle der Evangelisten* (Zürich, TVZ, 1972), pp. 96–7.

17 See H. Schürmann, 'Sprachliche Reminiszenzen an abgeänderte oder ausgelassene Bestandteile der Spruchsammlung im Lukas- und Matthäusevangelium', in *NTS*, 6 (1960), pp. 203–4. Matthew had in his version of Q equivalents of Luke 12.21 and 12.39 (note *thēsaurizōn*, *kleptēs*, *dioruchthēnai* and drew on these in reshaping Matthew 6.19. Degenhardt, op. cit., pp. 88ff. thinks 'treasure on earth' is due to Matthew's redaction. Matthew is closer to Jewish tradition here; see below. But Dupont, *Béatitudes*, III, 116 thinks Matthew 6.19 the older version.

18 B. S. Easton, *The Gospel according to St Luke*, pp. xxv–xxvii gives a list of words characteristic of L. F. Rehkopf, *Die Lukanische Sonderquelle*, WUNT (1959) attempted a list of *proto*-Lucan vocabulary (his L equals Q plus S); but see H. Schürmann, 'Protolukanische Spracheigentumlichkeiten?' in *BZ*, 5 (1961), pp. 266–86 for objections and difficulties here. It is easier to list what is *pre*-Lucan than to assign it to a source or combination of sources.

19 For the debate on this question see nn. 10, and 11 above, and Appendix C.

20 H. Greeven, *Das Hauptproblem der Sozialethik in der neueren Stoa und im Urchristentum* (NF 3.4) (Gütersloh, Bertelsmann, 1935), p. 83.

21 B. E. McCormick, 'The Social and Economic Background of Luke' (unpublished thesis in the Bodleian Library, Oxford, 1960), pp. 132–154; cf. also pp. 186–205.

22 McCormick, 'The Social and Economic Background of Luke', pp. 132–54.

23 Degenhardt, op. cit. (esp. pp. 214–22) thinks that Luke's emphasis on almsgiving was directed to Gentile Christians less accustomed to such teaching than Jewish Christians. He sees the teaching addressed to disciples as aimed at the church officials of his time, forbidding a concern for gain and encouraging them to renunciation and generosity. Degenhardt's work contains many useful observations, but does not study quite all of the Lucan redaction. It is not clear that references to disciples are always to be referred to church officials. It is

also likely that the emphasis on almsgiving and renunciation which we find in the Third Gospel owes more to Luke's *sources* than Degenhardt seems to envisage.

24 J. R. Michaels, 'Apostolic Hardships and Righteous Gentiles, a Study of Matthew 25.31–46', in *JBL*, 84 (1965), pp. 27–37; L. Cope, 'Matthew 25.31–46, "The Sheep and Goats" Reinterpreted', in *Nov. T.*, xi (1969), pp. 32–44; J. Manek, 'Mit wem identifiziert sich Jesus (Matt. 25.31–46)?' In *Christ and Spirit in the New Testament*, ed. B. Lindars and S. S. Smalley (Cambridge, Cambridge University Press, 1973), pp. 15–25. Matthew 25.35–40 contains echoes of Isaiah 58.7 and Proverbs 19.17: what is done for the poor is done for the Lord. The Christian community saw itself as 'the poor'.

25 The versions given in Thomas are not necessarily prior. One should not press unduly the incidental details in parables. Interpreters differ over the point of these parables; see the more detailed discussion below.

26 W. G. Kümmel, *Introduction to the New Testament*, p. 98 lists the suggestions.

27 On the redaction of Mark 10 see E. Best, 'The Camel and the Needle's Eye', in *Exp Tim*, 82 (1970), pp. 83–9; E. Schweizer, *The Good News according to Mark* (SPCK 1971), p. 209. Légasse, *L'Appel du riche*, pp. 64–76 thinks that a saying like Matthew 7.13–14 lies behind Mark 10.24. Though Légasse differs in his reconstruction of the development, he agrees that severity in the middle stage is later relaxed.

28 On the ecclesiastical vocabulary and setting of Mark 4.13–20 see Schweizer, *Mark*, p. 96; V. Taylor, *The Gospel according to St Mark* (Macmillan 1957), p. 261. On the vocabulary of Mark 7.22 see Taylor, op. cit., p. 347.

29 H. C. Kee, *Community of the New Age* (SCM Press 1977), pp. 90–91.

30 See n. 2 above.

31 D. Lührmann, *Die Redaktion der Logienquelle* (WMANT) (Neukirchener Verlag 1969); P. Hoffmann, *Studien zur Theologie der Logienquelle* (N.T.Abh. 8) (Münster, Aschendorff, [2]1972); R. A. Edwards, *A Theology of Q* (Philadelphia, Fortress, 1976); and the commentary by S. Schulz, *Q, Die Spruchquelle der Evangelisten.*

32 See esp. Psalms 9.18–21; 10.12–18; 14.5–7; 69.33–7; 147.6 (in all of which the context suggests a national reference). This motif reappears in Ps. Sol. 5.2, 11; 15.2; 18.2, and in the Scrolls of the Qumran sect in 1Q Hod. 2.32; 3.25; 5.13–22; 18.14 (cf. 17.26, with echoes of Isaiah 61.1), 4Q p Ps. 37.21–2, 1Q Mil. 11.13. Of the extensive secondary literature see esp. E. Percy, *Die Botschaft Jesu*, pp. 53–4, 63–4, 81; S. Mowinckel, *The Psalms in Israel's Worship* (Oxford, Blackwell, 1962), I, pp. 223n, 208ff., 229; II, pp. 91–2, 251; E. Bammel, *TDNT*, 6, pp. 888–99; L. E. Keck, 'The Poor among the Saints in Jewish Christianity and Qumran', in *ZNW*, 57 (1966), pp. 68–75. See also Appendix B.

33 M. Weber, *The Sociology of Religion* (Methuen 1965), pp. 108–16; C. Y. Glock, 'The Role of Deprivation in the Origin and Evolution of Religious Groups', in R. Lee and M. E. Marty, *Religion and Social Conflict* (New York, Oxford University Press, 1964), pp. 24–36. Note

the role of persecution in the last of the four beatitudes which presumably formed a group in Q.

34 See Kümmel, op. cit., p. 66.

35 See discussion of Mark 6.8–9 above. On the whole question of wandering prophets see G. Theissen, 'Wanderradikalismus', in *ZTK*, 70 (1973), pp. 245–71.

36 Luke 16.13 par., Matt. 6.24 (though the preceding verses in Luke lack a parallel in Matthew). For mammon see Ecclesiasticus 31.8 (Heb.), 1QS 6.2, ZD 14.20, and references to the Targum in Hauck, *TDNT*, 4, pp. 388–9.

37 Cf. Matt. 6.19–20 and Luke 12.33–4, but the versions differ in other respects. For the Jewish contrast of earthly and heavenly treasure see BB 11a; J. Pea 1.1.15b (53); Tos. Pea 4.18 (24); Pesik. R.25 (126b). Matthew is closer to the Jewish version; see below.

38 Cf. Lührmann, *Redaktion der Logenquelle*, 84; W. L. Knox, *The Sources of the Synoptic Gospels* (Cambridge 1957), II, pp. 66ff.

39 See n. 18 above.

40 On this question see esp. H. Schürmann, 'Sprachliche Reminiszenzen', in *NTS*, 6, pp. 193–210.

41 Cf. H. Schürmann, *Lukas*, I, pp. 75–9.

42 See n. 32 above for references to the Psalms, Ps. Sol. and 1Q Hod.

43 Schürmann, *Lukas*, I, p. 169 argues that it is a Lucan redaction of pre-Lucan material possibly from Q.

44 Schürmann, op. cit., pp. 221–59, esp. pp. 241–2.

45 Details in Schürmann, op. cit., pp. 336–41.

46 In addition to the references to Psalms, Ps. Sol. and 1Q Hod. in n. 32 above, there is the reversal theology of the admonitions of Enoch. See 1 Enoch 94–104, where we find fierce resentment directed at wealthy persecutors. The oppressors are rich (94.8; 96.4; 97.8; 98.2–3; 102.9) and appear to be righteous (96.4) but they build in sin, unrighteousness, and deceit (94.6–7). They eat and drink well, tread down the lowly, and oppress the righteous (96.5–8, cf. 95.7). They plunder, and sin, and rob (102.9), and murder, but remain unpunished by the rulers (103.12–15). The author predicts that they will lose their riches (94.8; 97.10), they and their goods will perish (98.2–3). The argument that righteous and wicked die alike, without retribution, is rebutted; joy awaits the righteous, but the sinners will suffer fire and torment (103.2–7, cf. Wisdom 2.1—5.23). The expectation of a reversal of fortune hereafter arises from a keen sense of resentment. The persecuted had expected to become the head, and had become the tail (103.11). Luke 1.53 is much less severe than 1 Enoch 94–104, but Luke 6.24–6 and 16.19–31 are closer in spirit. For early Christian reversal theology see also James 5.1–6 and Revelation 18, the latter reflecting an era of persecution. On the role of resentment in Judaism and Christianity see the savage comments in F. Nietzsche, *The Antichrist*, paras 24, 43, 45, 51. (Liable to be misunderstood unless his personal opposition to anti-Semitism is remembered.) Max Weber developed the understanding of religious resentment, although he says more about the psalms and much less about the New Testament; see

M. Weber, *Sociology of Religion*, pp. 110–16. Further discussion below. On *peripeteia* in Hellenistic literature, and on the teaching of Jewish Wisdom literature that change of fortune is in the hands of God, see Dupont, *Béatitudes*, III, pp. 186, n. 1 and 192, n. 3.

47 Schürmann, *Lukas*, I, pp. 336–41. On the question of vocabulary see also Degenhardt, *Lukas*, pp. 51–3. For a quite different view see Dupont, *Béatitudes* ²I, pp. 299–342 and III, pp. 30–97.

48 In favour of attribution to Q see Easton, *Luke*, XXI and 201. See also Schürmann, 'Sprachliche Reminiszenzen', p. 203 for the view that Matthew 6.19 echoes the wording found in Luke 12.21.

49 Assigned to M and Q in T. W. Manson, *The Sayings of Jesus* (SCM Press 1954), pp. 114, 172; to Q and L in Easton, *Luke*, p. 204; alteration by Luke according to J. M. Creed, *The Gospel according to St Luke* (Macmillan 1930), p. 175; possibly weakening by Matthew according to F. W. Beare, *Earliest Records of Jesus* (Oxford, Blackwell, 1964), p. 169. Though Luke does destroy parallelism, Matthew sometimes improves on the poetry he inherits from Mark; cf. Goulder, *Midrash and Lection*, pp. 70–92. In this passage Matthew seems to have improved the poetry and diluted the message.

50 On the hortatory expansion and addition see J. Jeremias, *The Parables of Jesus* (SCM Press 1972), pp. 44–5; on the Lucan vocabulary of verse 12 see Degenhardt, *Lukas*, p. 101, n. 11. The parable in the Gospel of Thomas 64 is different again, and expresses hostility to traders and merchants.

51 R. Bultmann, *History of the Synoptic Tradition* (Eng. trans. Oxford, Blackwell, 1963), p. 170 regards verse 33 as secondary expansion of the parable. 'Every one of you' (v. 33) may echo 'which of you' in verse 28, and 'cannot be my disciple' echoes 14.26–7, but 14.33 may still have been part of whichever source Luke is here following. Degenhardt, *Lukas*, p. 111 thinks the Hellenistic formulation points to Luke, but that is not necessarily the case.

52 Jeremias, op. cit., p. 182; cf. L. J. Topel, 'On the Injustice of the Unjust Steward', in *CBQ* 37 (1975), pp. 216–27.

53 Dupont, *Béatitudes*, III, pp. 168–72 notes in verse 11 'unrighteous mammon' opposed to 'the true' and parallel to 'that which is another's', i.e. that which belongs to God.

54 Opposition to wealth and unjust gain: 1QS 9.21–2, 10.19; ZD 4.17, 6.15–16; Hod. 10.23, 10.30. More specific charges against men of injustice: 1QS 11.2; ZD 8.5–7; 1Q p Hab. 12.2–10; cf. I. Hahn, 'Die Eigentumsverhältnisse der Qumran Sekte', in *Wiss. Zeitschrift*, 12 (1963), pp. 263–6.

55 *hyparchontes* and compounds with *phil-* being Lucan: Dupont, *Béatitudes*, III, p. 63. But see Schürmann, 'Sprachliche Reminiszenzen', pp.200–210.

56 Cf. G. Zilboorg, *Psychoanalysis and Religion* (Allen & Unwin 1967), pp. 72–3, on accusations of this nature.

57 Dupont, op. cit., pp. 173–82; Degenhardt, *Lukas*, p. 133.

58 Bultmann, *Tradition*, pp. 33–4; Braun, *Radikalismus*, II, p. 27n.

59 H. Schürmann, *Jesu Abshiedsrede Lk. 22.21–38* (NTAbh) (Münster, Aschendorff, 1957), pp. 116–39.

60 Jeremias, *Theology*, I, p. 294 attributes the saying to Jesus; Manson, *Sayings*, p. 341 thinks the remark ironic; Easton, *Luke*, pp. 328–9 holds that Jesus wished to ensure the escape of his disciples. S. G. F. Brandon, *Jesus and the Zealots* (Manchester University Press 1967), pp. 203, 340, 355, n. 3 thinks Jesus ensured that his disciples were armed. A sword was used in Gethsemane. Beare, *Records*, p. 229 speaks of stray Zealot phrases intruding their way into the gospel record.

61 See above, nn. 32 and 46. On apocalyptic Christian polemic see also Hengel, *Property and Riches*, pp. 46–9.

CHAPTER THREE
Hostility to Wealth in the Oral Tradition

1 On this question see D. L. Mealand, 'The Dissimilarity Test', in *SJT*, 31 (1978), pp. 41–50.

2 Cf. D. L. Mealand, 'Community of Goods and Utopian Allusions in Acts II–IV', in *JTS*, 28 (1977), pp. 96–9.

3 Jos. Ant., 3.15 (320) discussed above.

4 Jos. Ant., 20.2 (51) cf. T. Pea 4.18.

5 See ch. 1 above.

6 N. J. Smelser, *Sociology of Economic Life* (Englewood Cliffs, Prentice Hall, 1963), p. 44.

7 Max Weber, *The Sociology of Religion*, p. 108.

8 Weber, op. cit., pp. 110–11. Modern secular examples are given in A. Lauterbach, *Man, Motives, and Money* (Ithaca NY, Cornell University Press, [2]1959), p. 47.

9 Weber, op. cit., pp. 110–26. Weber speaks of the resentment of a pariah group: a distinctive and exclusive, but subject and disprivileged group. He followed Nietzsche in finding this in Jewish texts such as the psalms (p. 111) but resists Nietzsche's application of the same principle to the NT. Nietzsche's attack was certainly indiscriminate, but Weber has to admit the existence of a doctrine of compensation in the story of Dives and Lazarus (p. 115). Weber goes on to point out that disprivilege in itself does not always produce resentment, nor are all forms of salvation religion to be ascribed to this source. The role of *relative* disprivilege is emphasized in more recent studies. Cf. J. M. Yinger, *The Scientific Study of Religion* (Macmillan 1970), pp. 288–9, and n. 10 below.

10 C. Y. Glock, 'The Role of Deprivation in the Origin and Evolution of Religious Groups', pp. 24–36; N. Cohn, *The Pursuit of the Millennium* (Paladin [2]1970), pp. 281–6; W. Stark, *Sociology of Religion*, II (Routledge & Kegan Paul 1966), pp. 5, 51. On the revolutionary element in modern messianic movements see V. Lanternari, *The Religions of the Oppressed* (New York, Mentor, 1965), pp. 239–54.

11 Glock, op. cit., pp. 24–36.

12 G. Zilboorg, *Psychoanalysis and Religion* (Allen & Unwin 1967), pp. 72–3.

13 For a longer list of relevant passages see ch. 2, n. 32 and n. 46. See also Wisdom 2.6—5.23, esp. 2.6, 5.8.

14 Cf. D. R. Dudley, *A History of Cynicism* (Methuen 1937), pp. 79–80.

15 1 Enoch 5.7 (2 Enoch 52); Sukka 56b; Yoma 87a; cf. Bultmann, *Tradition*, pp. 111–12. On Eccles. 10.16–17, 1 En. 99.10–15, s Apoc. Bar. 10.6–7, Ber. 61b, etc. see Dupont, *Béatitudes*, 1, pp. 326–35.

16 For woes see Mark 13.17; 14.21; Matthew 11.21 par.

17 See ch. 2 above, and ch. 2, n. 15.

18 So Guelich, 'Matthean Beatitudes' (1976), p. 417; E. Schweizer, 'Formgeschichtliches zu den Seligpreisungen Jesu', in *NTS*, 19 (1973), p. 122.

19 Schürmann, *Lukas*, p. 346.

20 See above, esp. n. 13. A similarity with 1 Corinthians 4.8 is noted by J. M. Robinson, *A New Quest of the Historical Jesus* (SCM Press 1959), p. 123.

21 In the case of some of the psalms there is the background of a small nation oppressed by larger empires. The Admonitions of Enoch and 1Q Hodayoth reflect tensions within Judaism. Wisdom 2–5 may reflect the problems of Alexandrian Jews. The Psalms of Solomon and the War Scroll seem to reflect both sectarian and wider conflicts. Further discussion is beyond the scope of the present work but reference may be made to O. Eissfeldt, *The Old Testament* (Oxford, Blackwell, 1966), pp. 600–602, 610–13, 619, 652–4.

22 Jos. Ant., 20.2.5 (49–53).

23 Jos. Ant., 20.9.1 (199–200).

24 Percy, *Botschaft*, pp. 94–5, 100. But see also E. Pax, 'Der Reiche und der arme Lazarus. Eine Milieustudie', in *Studii Biblici Franciscani Liber Annuus*, 25 (1975), pp. 254–68.

25 On the social structure of the time see Jeremias, *Jerusalem*, pp. 87–119, 228–32; Kreissig, *Sozialen Zusammenhänge*, pp. 82–7; and ch. 1 above.

26 Jeremias, *Parables*, pp. 182–3; Degenhardt, *Lukas*, p. 113.

27 Jeremias, *Parables*, p. 38.

28 1 Enoch 103.5–8; 104.4 (trans. Charles), cf. Wisdom 2.21ff.

29 See j. Hag. 2, 77d, 38. Both versions of the story are retold in T. W. Manson, *The Sayings of Jesus*, p. 297. See also Jeremias, op. cit., p. 183; Creed, *Luke*, pp. 208–10.

30 Percy, *Botschaft*, pp. 97–9 rightly notes the difference between the more complex rabbinic beliefs about rewards and Luke 16.19–31.

31 One could also compare 'You ... received your good things' (Luke 16.25) with 'For you have received your consolation' (Luke 6.24), but see also Matthew 6.5.

32 Beare, *Records*, pp. 182–3 is critical of Manson, *Sayings*, p. 297, who sees the parable as directed by *Jesus* against the Sadducees. But Manson may have been partly right. The Sadducees may well be the

target, even if the story comes from the early Church. Attempts by others to find allusions to the Gentile question are far-fetched.

33 So correctly Beare, *Records*, p. 183. Bultmann, *Tradition*, p. 203 notes the considerable debt to Judaism. The idea that Moses and the prophets preach resurrection could have come from Judaism, but is Christian in its present setting, with its reference to someone rising from the dead.

34 The rich man is a 'son of Abraham'.

35 Braun, *Radikalismus*, p. 74, n. 4 describes the parable as Lucan, but it is pre-Lucan. It is closer to 1 Enoch 94–104 than to Qumran. Degenhardt, *Lukas*, p. 135 thinks that Luke 16.14–31 is directed against libertine gnostics of Luke's day. This is not necessarily so. Luke has retained older material reflecting resentment of the Sadducees.

36 For contrast between God and the world see 2 Corinthians 6.14–15; James 4.4; 1 John 2.15.

37 So E. Haenchen, *Der Weg Jesu* (Berlin, Töpelmann, 1966), p. 358.

38 So C. F. Burney, *The Poetry of Our Lord* (Oxford, Clarendon Press, 1925), p. 115; cf. M. Black, *An Aramaic Approach to the Gospels and Acts* (Oxford, Clarendon Press, [3]1967, p. 178 on other poetic features.

39 Redactional according to Degenhardt, *Lukas*, pp. 88–9; shaped liturgically according to Kilpatrick, *Origin of Matthew*, p. 75.

40 Burney, op. cit., pp. 87–8, 115. Black, op. cit., p. 178, finds paronomasia in Luke 12.33c, 34. Some source critics assigned the two versions to different sources.

41 H. Montefiore and H. E. W. Turner, *Thomas and the Evangelists* (SCM Press 1962), p. 67, cf. R. McL. Wilson, *Studies in the Gospel of Thomas* (Mowbray 1960), pp. 92–3; both are cautious about the derivation of the saying.

42 Kümmel, *Introduction*, p. 66. W. Pesch, 'Zur Exegese von Mt. 6.19–21 und Lk. 12.33–4', in *Biblica*, 41 (1960), p. 360 puts too much weight on Luke 12.32.

43 See ch. 2, n. 17 above.

44 On this issue see Mealand, 'Dissimilarity Test', *passim*.

45 Cf. Ecclus. 29.10f.; Ep. Jer. 12; Wisdom 5.8–9; 1 Enoch 97.9–10. Hoarding treasure is contrasted with alms in Tobit 12.8. James 5.2–3 also mentions moth and rust. His suggestion that gold rusts only reveals how little opportunity the author had to possess such wealth.

46 Ps. Sol. 9.9; 2 Enoch 50.5, cf. 4 Ezra 6.5; 7.77; 2 Bar. 14.12.

47 Ecclus. 29.10, Jos. and Asenath 12–13, T. Job 36 (cf. also 33). For the contrast of corruptible and incorruptible see 2 Bar. 74.2; 85.4–5. Most important is T. Pea 4.18 par. discussed in the text.

48 Pesch, 'Zur Exegese von Mt. 6.19', p. 366 cites few examples and minimizes their relevance. He overstates his case in excluding the idea of reward, which is clearly suggested by 'treasure in heaven'. His emphasis on the uniqueness and importance of Matthew 6.21 par. misses the point that it is probably an independent logion (so Braun, *Radikalismus*, II, p. 74, n. 2), and is not so very unusual, cf. T. Job 36.

49 Cited by Preisker in *TDNT*, 4.715.

50 Braun, op. cit., p. 77, n. 1.

51 Even if the last few words of 12.15 are Lucan (so Degenhardt, *Lukas*, p. 74), they do not alter the sense. In Luke 12.21 to be 'rich before God' means to give alms: Easton, *Luke*, p. 201. Though some manuscripts omit verse 21 it is probably derived from Luke's source; see Degenhardt, *Lukas*, p. 79, cf. Bultmann, *Tradition*, p. 361. The source may well be Q, see above. On the secondary nature of the version in Thomas see H. Schürmann, *Traditionsgeschichtlichen Untersuchungen zu den synoptischen Evangelien* (Düsseldorf, Patmos, 1968), pp. 233, 246 (= *BZ* 7 (1963)).

52 Cf. Ecclus. 11.18–19; 1 Enoch 97.8–10. See also Bultmann, *Tradition*, pp. 97, 204, 394 for parallels from other literature.

53 Jeremias, *Parables*, p. 165. Degenhardt, *Lukas*, p. 78 thinks the parable is aimed at those who delay a decision for the Kingdom, which also presupposes an eschatological interpretation.

54 Bultmann, op. cit., pp. 87, 91.

55 Thomas log. 48. On the proverb see Jeremias, *Parables*, p. 194, and Manson, *Sayings*, p. 133.

56 1QS 6.2; CD 14.20; 1Q 27.1.2.5; cf. Hauck, *TDNT*, 4, pp. 388–90, and Black, op. cit., pp. 139–40.

57 Braun, *Radikalismus*, II, pp. 74, 78; Légasse, *L'Appel du riche*, p. 164. J. D. M. Derrett, 'Fresh Light on St Luke XVI', in *NTS*, 7 (1961), p. 218 relies too much on the assumption that the context is an original unit.

58 Even Légasse, op. cit., p. 163, who objects to this common view, speaks on p. 164 of 'un anti-Dieu'.

59 See Colossians 3.5; Ephesians 5.5 (unless lust is meant here, cf. Taylor, *Mark*, p. 345); cf. T. Jud. 19.1–2.

60 Bion of Borysthenes: 'He has not acquired property, it has acquired him', DL 4.50. See also Eur. Hecuba 864; further examples in J. J. Wetstein, *Novum Testamentum Graecum* (Amsterdam, I, 1751), p. 333. Manson, *Sayings*, p. 133 cites Plato *Rep*. 8.555c, and Persius *Sat*. 5.154ff.

61 Chaeremon *apud* Porph. *Abst*. 4.6.

62 *plousion* W c, *tous pepoithotas epi* (*tois* DΘ f1 f13) *chrēmasin* A C K XΠDΘ f1 f13 it b d ff^{2} Clem. etc., *hoi ta chrēmata echontes* 1241, *qui pecunias habent vel confidentes in eis:* a. See Clement of Alexandria, *Quis Dives Salvetur*, 4 (938P).

63 א B Δ Ψ it k.

64 Taylor, *Mark*, pp. 431–2 prefers the order of D a b d ff^{2}, but see Légasse, *L'Appel du riche*, pp. 74–5, n. 26.

65 Against Wellhausen and Klostermann on this point see Bultmann, *Tradition*, p. 22 (against J. Wellhausen, *Das Evangelium Marci* (Berlin, Reimer, ^{2}1909), 81 (only in the second edition)).

66 N. Walter, 'Zur Analyse von Mc 10.17–31', in *ZNW*, 53 (1962), pp. 206–18. Others regard verses 23 and 25 as the original unit: cf.

Bultmann, *Tradition*, p. 22; Braun, *Radikalismus*, II, p. 75; E. Best, 'The Camel and the Needle's Eye', pp. 83–9.

67 H. W. Kuhn, *Ältere Sammlungen in Markusevangelium* (Göttingen, Vandenhoeck u. Ruprecht, 1971), p. 172; W. Harnisch, 'Die Berufung des Reichen. Zur Analyse von Markus 10.17–27', in *Festschrift für E. Fuchs*, eds G. Ebeling *et al.* (Tübingen, Mohr, 1973), pp. 161–176.

68 B. M. 38b, cf. Berak. 55b; see also Midr. Song of Songs 5.2: 'Present to me an opening of repentance no bigger than the eye of a needle, and I will widen it into openings through which wagons and carriages can pass' (trans. M. Simon).

69 For details see Taylor, *Mark*, p. 431.

70 For antecedents in the Hebrew Bible see N. Perrin, *The Kingdom of God in the Teaching of Jesus* (SCM Press 1963), p. 184. Further examples from the gospels include Mark 10.15; Matthew 5.20; 7.21; John 3.5. On the demands made by *Jesus* see pp. 78–82.

71 Degenhardt, *Lukas*, pp. 27–41. But in other contexts it is clear that such instructions were given specifically to wandering missionaries. See below on Mark 6.8 par. and also Theissen, 'Wanderradikalismus', p. 252.

72 But see Degenhardt, *Lukas*, p. 111.

73 Bornhäuser, *Der Christ und seine Habe*, p. 42.

74 In addition to the works cited in ch. 2, n. 24 see also Theissen, 'Wanderradikalismus', p. 255.

75 D. R. A. Hare, *The Theme of Jewish Persecution in the Gospel according to St Matthew* (Cambridge University Press 1967), p. 124, though he cites doctrinal and moral objections rather than historical and exegetical ones. Such considerations should follow rather than precede proper exegesis.

76 Ezek. 18.7; Tobit 4.16; Sota 14a; Ned. 40a; Sheb. 35b.

77 Eg. Book of the Dead 125; Homer *Od.* 9.270; Cic. *Off.* 2.18.

CHAPTER FOUR
Poverty and the Kingdom of God
Jesus and his disciples

1 See ch. 2 above and ch. 2, nn. 5–9.

2 On the tendencies of the Matthean redaction see J. Rohde, *Rediscovering the Teaching of the Evangelists* (SCM Press 1968), pp. 47–112, and the works cited there.

3 It is theoretically possible to see Matthew's beatitudes as directed to those who lack righteousness, mourn their sins, and are spiritually needy (Matt. 5.6; 5.4; 5.3). But such an interpretation conflicts with the overall plan of the Matthean beatitudes. See Percy, *Botschaft*, p. 43; Degenhardt, *Lukas*, pp. 49ff.; Dupont, *Béatitudes*, I, pp. 221–2; Dupont, 'Introduction aux Béatitudes', pp. 103–7.

4 See ch. 2 and ch. 3 above.

5 See N. Perrin, *Rediscovering the Teaching of Jesus* (SCM Press 1967), pp. 253–4 who lists opinions on the matter.

6 Bultmann, *Tradition*, p. 110; Dupont, *Béatitudes* ²II, pp. 380–81.

7 Schürmann, *Lukas*, p. 329 gives a list which includes Wellhausen, Streeter, Dibelius, Manson, Grundmann, and Black for the second person; Harnack, Klostermann, Bultmann, Daube, and Dupont for the third person.

8 D. Daube, *The New Testament and Rabbinic Judaism* (Athlone Press 1956), pp. 196–201.

9 E. Käsemann, *New Testament Questions of Today* (SCM Press 1969), pp. 100–101 suggests that all the beatitudes may be the products of early Christian prophecy. W. G. Kümmel, *Promise and Fulfilment* (SCM Press 1957), p. 49 rightly expresses caution about the temporal reference of the beatitudes. E. Fuchs, *Studies of the Historical Jesus* (SCM Press 1964), p. 224 speaks of those summoned by Jesus in the beatitudes as 'men who had everything to expect from God and nothing more from the world'.

10 See Dupont, 'Introduction aux Béatitudes', pp. 99–101, 107; Dupont, *Béatitudes* ²II, pp. 379–80.

11 Often understood in a figurative sense (*Str-B* 1.596) but here intended literally.

12 Heb. *'anāwîm*, humble; but humble status as well as humble outlook may be implied. (LXX *ptōchois*). See Appendix B.

13 Jub. 23.26–31; 1 Enoch 5.8–9; 25.5–6; 96.3; Sib. Or. 3.367–80, and later sources listed in *Str-B* 1.594.

14 Jeremias, *Parables*, p. 177.

15 Pea 1.1, cf. G. F. Moore, *Judaism* (Cambridge, Mass., Harvard University Press, 1927), II, pp. 89–92, 322 (esp. p. 92).

16 1 Enoch 102–3; Wisdom 2–3, 5.1ff., cf. also 4Q p Ps. 37, and other passages discussed above.

17 Galatians 2.10, cf. Romans 15.26, and the expectations implied in the grouping of beatitudes and woes in the pre-Lucan tradition. In 4Q p Ps. 37, col. 1, the *ᵃnāwîm* of the psalm are interpreted as the [community] of the poor (*'ebyônîm*).

18 Bultmann, *Tradition*, pp. 126, 128, 151, followed by R. H. Fuller, *Interpreting the Miracles* (SCM Press 1966), pp. 27–8. See also Kümmel, *Promise and Fulfilment*, pp. 109–11; J. Jeremias, *New Testament Theology*, I (SCM Press 1971), pp. 103–21, and Schürmann, *Lukas*, p. 414.

19 Jeremias, *N. T. Theology*, I, pp. 114–21; Fuchs, *Studies*, pp. 20–21.

20 E. Linnemann, *Parables of Jesus* (SPCK 1966), pp. 88–92.

21 F. W. Beare, 'The Mission of the Disciples and the Mission Charge', in *JBL*, 89 (1970), pp. 1–13; cf. F. Hahn, *Mission in the New Testament* (SCM Press 1965), p. 41. See also Hoffmann, *Theologie der Logienquelle*, pp. 264–314. (Manson, *Sayings*, p. 257 ascribed it to L.)

22 Did. 12.2; 11.10–12. On the possibilities of exploitation see the biting

remarks of Lucian in Peregrinus 11–13. On the whole question see Theissen, 'Wanderradikalismus', pp. 245–53, 263.

23 Beare, 'Mission', pp. 1–13; Hahn, *Mission*, p. 41.

24 On this see J. Jeremias, 'Paarweise Sendung im NT' in *New Testament Essays*, ed. A. J. B. Higgins (Manchester University Press 1959), pp. 136–43. On the problems of reconstructing the text of Q see Hoffmann, *Theologie der Logienquelle*, pp. 248, 264, 267.

25 See also Acts 13.51; 18.6. Those who reject the message of the Kingdom are regarded as no part of the true Israel; cf. Manson, *Sayings*, p. 76.

26 Cf. Beare, 'Mission', pp. 10–13, Hahn, *Mission*, p. 46. For rabbinic rules on the subject see Ar. 16b; the only approved reason for changing lodgings was the suffering of physical violence.

27 For rabbinic passages see Jeb. 16.7, BB 133b. A rough cloak, a staff, and a begging bag were the usual Cynic garb; cf. Epictetus 3.22.10. (Josephus says the Essenes took nothing with them except that they were armed as protection against brigands, BJ.2.124–7.)

28 R. Pesch, *Das Markusevangelium*, 1 (Freiburg, Herder, 1976), p. 328; cf. Hoffmann, *Theologie der Logienquelle*, pp. 324–6. (Mark 2.23 and 8.14 have been cited as evidence that Jesus and his disciples went hungry; Mark 12.15 and Matthew 17.27 that they carried no coins; but these are incidental details in narrative and not necessarily to be pressed, and in any case contrast John 12.6; 13.29.)

29 Ta'an 13a.

30 See Sabb.152a for insults to a rabbi who had no shoes.

31 Ber. 9.5; B. Ber. 62b; T. Ber. 7.19 (17); J. Ber. 9.8. Cf. Manson, *Sayings*, p. 181; Taylor, *Mark*, p. 304; Hengel, *Nachfolge*, p. 84, n. 146; Hoffmann, *Theologie der Logienquelle*, pp. 322–3.

32 Hahn, *Mission*, p. 45; Hoffmann, *Theologie der Logienquelle*, p. 298.

33 Berak. 5.1, also j. Berak. 5, 9a, 24, Berak. 14a, 32b, cf. Berak. 2.1 (one should not normally greet someone while reciting a section of the Shema').

34 See the acute observation of Theissen, 'Wanderradikalismus', p. 264.

35 D. L. Mealand, 'The Disparagement of Wealth in New Testament Times', diss. (Bristol 1971), pp. 355–72; G. Dautzenberg, 'Der Verzicht auf das apostolische Unterhaltsrecht. Eine exegetische Untersuchung zu 1 Kor 9', in *Biblica*, 50 (1969), pp. 212–32.

36 See L. Festinger *et al.*, *When Prophecy Fails* (New York, Harper, 1956), p. 28; L. Festinger, *A Theory of Cognitive Dissonance* (California, Stanford University Press, 1957), p. 18 is cited in J. G. Gager, *Kingdom and Community* (Englewood Cliffs, Prentice Hall, 1975), p. 39.

37 Menippus the satirist mentioned in DL 6.99f. was from Gadara, as was the Cynic poet Meleagar, and later Oenomaus of Gadara, who was possibly known to the rabbis; cf. Dudley, *History of Cynicism*, p. 162. See also M. Hadas, 'Gadarenes in Pagan Literature', in *Classical Weekly*, 25 (1931), pp. 25–30. The Epicurean Philodemus of Gadara opposed Cynic renunciation of property, but himself only

advocated such wealth as is necessary for the philosopher, cf. pap. 339, cols 9ff., *De Oeconomia* cols 11–12. Coastal cities such as Tyre, Sidon, and Ascalon produced philosophers of note, such as Antiochus of Ascalon.

38 On Diogenes' legendary simplicity of life see DL 6.22, 23, 37, 46, 49, 70–71. He lived in a tub, or in temples, or other public buildings, inured himself to heat and cold, was not averse to begging, and is said to have carried self-sufficiency so far as to throw away his cup after seeing a child drink from its hands. For tales about how Crates gave away his possessions see DL 6.87–8. On the early Cynics see Dudley, *Cynicism*, pp. 27–42. On the Roman Cynic Demetrius see Seneca, *De Ben.*, 7.11; *V. Beat.*, 18.3.

39 See Dio Chrys., *Or.* 32.9, though Dio himself lived for several years as a poor itinerant philosopher; cf. *Or.* 13. (He wandered as an exile wearing a rough cloak and was taken for a tramp, a beggar, or a philosopher: *Or.* 7.9; 33.14; 34.2; 72.2.) See also Epictetus 3.22; Philo *Fug.* 33.

40 Hoffman, *Theologie der Logienquelle*, pp. 240–41, 319; cf. Hengel, *Nachfolge*, pp. 36, 84–5.

41 Despite the efforts of E. Wechssler, *Hellas im Evangelium* (Hamburg, von Schröder, ^{2}1947) pp. 227–50; cf. Hengel, op. cit., pp. 59–60.

42 Hahn, *Mission*, p. 46; cf. Hengel, op. cit., pp. 84–5.

43 See n. 33 above.

44 Pesch, *Markusevangelium*, p. 328; Hoffmann, *Theologie der Logienquelle*, p. 327. See also below on Matthew 6.25–32 par.

45 See ch. 2, n. 59, also Jeremias, *New Testament Theology*, 1, p. 294, though he thinks that it goes back to Jesus. On the passage see also Conzelmann, *Theology of Luke*, pp. 81–3, 106–7.

46 H. Schürmann, *Jesu Abschiedsrede* pp. 116–36 gives detailed analysis of vocabulary and argues that Luke redacted a pre-Lucan tradition here. See also H. W. Bartsch, 'Jesu Schwertwort, Lukas XXII.35–8 Überlieferungsgeschichtliche Studie' in *NTS*, 20 (1973–4), pp. 190–203.

47 M. Smith, *Clement of Alexandria and a Secret Gospel of Mark* (Cambridge, Mass., Harvard University Press, 1973), pp. 448–53.

48 Recent studies include W. Zimmerli, 'Die Frage des Reichen nach dem ewigen Leben', in *Ev. T*, 19 (1959), pp. 90–97; Walter, 'Analyse von Mk. 10.17–31', pp. 206–18; Degenhardt, *Lukas*, pp. 136–49; Légasse, *L'Appel du riche*, *passim*, esp. pp. 50–57; Keck, 'Poor among the Saints', pp. 115–16; W. Harnisch, 'Die Berufung des Reichen', pp. 161–76.

49 For example one could compare Mark 6.4 with Plutarch, *De Exilio* 604 D, and Dio Chrys., *Or.* 47.6. With Mark 2.17 compare DL 6.6 and Dio Chrys., *Or.* 8.5.

50 Ket. 50a, cf. j. Pea 1.1.15b. The limit of a fifth was derived from the idiomatic repetition, 'Tithing I shall tithe' in Gen. 28.22. See also Arak. 8.4; Lev. R. 30.1; Ex. R. 47.5; Pesikta 178b.

51 A.Z. 64a.

52 BB 11a; J. Pea 1.1.15b (53); T. Pea 4.18 (24); Pesik. R. 25 (126b). His gifts to the Temple are mentioned in Yoma 3.10. See also Jos. Ant., 20.2.5 (51–3), and the discussion of Matthew 6.19–20 above; also ch. 1, n. 33 above.

53 Deut. 20.5–8, 1 Macc. 3.56; 2 Macc. 8.14, cf. M. Hengel, *Die Zeloten*, AGJU, (Leiden, Brill, ^{2}1976), pp. 255–6; Hengel, *Nachfolge*, pp. 21–3.

54 D. L. Mealand, 'Community of Goods at Qumran', *Theol. Zeitschr.*, 31 (1975), 129–39.

55 H. Braun, *Qumran und das Neue Testament* (Tübingen, Mohr, 1966), 1, pp. 143–9. (He also discusses earlier literature on this question.)

56 Acts suggests that, at first, efforts were made to assist the poor within the Church (Acts 2.45; 4.34; 4.36—5.11; 6.1). Later the Jerusalem Church itself needed help (Acts 11.28–30; Gal. 2.10). Mark 10.28–30 might well reflect the compensations offered by common life in the Church.

57 E. Schweizer, *Church Order in the New Testament* (SCM Press 1961) (2f) p. 27 rightly says it is no verbatim report. Fuchs, *Studies*, p. 149 includes Mark 10.21 in a list of sayings reflecting later hardship. Légasse, *L'Appel du riche*, 50–63, and others find a substantial historical core. Bultmann, *Tradition*, p. 55 argued that it was historical in that it gave fitting expression to Jesus's spiritual attitude.

58 Mean and ungenerous according to the Gospel of the Hebrews, cf. Hennecke, *NT Apocrypha*, 1, p. 149. He had made wealth an idol and so broken the first commandment: C. E. B. Cranfield, *The Gospel according to Saint Mark* (Cambridge University Press 1963), pp. 327–30. L. H. Marshall, *The Challenge of New Testament Ethics* (Macmillan 1966), p. 132 thinks Jesus wished to cure the man's selfishness.

59 Many see the demand as a special case. Cf. R. Schnackenburg, *The Moral Teaching of the New Testament* (Freiburg and London, Herder, 1965), p. 50; Légasse, op. cit., pp. 50–55.

60 Percy, *Botschaft*, pp. 92–3, argues against this limitation to a smaller group.

61 With C. K. Barrett, *Jesus and the Gospel Tradition* (SPCK 1967), pp. 46–9, 84–7, 105–8, against Perrin, *Teaching*, pp. 202–6. See also Kümmel, *Promise*, pp. 152–5.

62 See above.

63 Percy, *Botschaft*, p. 93; but see Hengel, *Nachfolge*, p. 68.

64 Luke 5.11; cf. John 21.1–11.

65 Taylor, *Mark*, p. 167; Bultmann, *Tradition*, p. 28 (also as the condensation of a process, p. 58); Pesch, *Markus*, p. 108. See also Hengel, op. cit., p. 5, n. 14, and R. Pesch, 'Berufung und Sendung', in *ZKT*, 91 (1969), pp. 1–31. Further literature in Pesch, *Markus*, p. 116.

66 Hengel, op. cit., p. 5; Pesch, 'Berufung', pp. 11–12; Pesch, *Markus*, p. 113.

67 See the discussion of Matthew 8.19–22 par., below.

68 Pesch, 'Berufung', pp. 18ff.; Pesch, *Markus*, p. 109, where reference

is also made to the stories about the call of Moses, Gideon, Samuel, and Saul.

69 A. Vööbus, *History of Asceticism in the Syrian Orient* (Louvain, CSCO, 184.14, 1958), I, pp. 1–30; E. Peterson, *Frühkirche Judentum und Gnosis* (Freiburg, Herder, 1959), pp. 209–20; G. Kretschmar, 'Ein Beitrag zur Frage nach dem Ursprung frühchristlicher Askese', pp. 32ff.; Theissen, 'Wanderradikalismus' *passim*.

70 For the metaphor see 1QH 5.8, and DL 4.16. Retranslation and further discussion in Hengel, *Nachfolge*, pp. 85–7; see also W. H. Wuellner, *The Meaning of 'Fishers of Men'* (Philadelphia 1967), pp. 160–63.

71 This point is sharply put by Gager, *Kingdom and Community*, pp. 37–49.

72 Hahn, *Mission*, pp. 46, 164.

73 Hengel, op. cit., pp. 21–37, 74.

74 G. Vermes, *Jesus the Jew* (Collins 1973), pp. 69–82.

75 Discussed above, but see also R. E. Brown, *The Gospel according to John* (Chapman 1971), II, pp. 1090–92 for the second view, and R. H. Fuller, *The Formation of the Resurrection Narratives* (SPCK 1972) for the former view.

76 Schürmann, *Lukas*, p. 273.

77 Nineham, *Mark*, p. 99.

78 Taylor, *Mark*, p. 204; Braun, *Radikalismus*, II, p. 76, n. 1; Pesch, *Markus*, p. 167.

79 Bab. Q. 10.1–2 (= Danby, *Mishnah*, p. 346). See also Luke 19.8 for extortion by tax collectors, and Matthew 5.46 for attitudes towards them.

80 The mission charge is the next Q passage after Matthew 8.22; see Kümmel, *Introduction*, p. 66.

81 Bultmann, *Tradition*, p. 28.

82 H. E. Tödt, *The Son of Man in the Synoptic Tradition* (SCM Press 1965), p. 122; F. Hahn, *The Titles of Jesus in Christology* (Lutterworth 1969), p. 36.

83 Fuchs, *Studies*, p. 149; Tödt, *Son of Man*, p. 122; Hahn, *Titles*, pp. 36–7.

84 Braun, *Radikalismus*, II, pp. 73–80; Schweizer, *Lordship and Discipleship* (SCM Press 1960), p. 16; see also Kümmel, *Promise*, p. 46.

85 See Manson, *Sayings*, p. 73; Bultmann, *Tradition*, p. 29.

86 Bultmann, *Tradition*, p. 105; Fuchs, *Studies*, p. 149; Hengel, *Nachfolge*, pp. 6–7, 16–17; see also Käsemann, *Essays*, pp. 37–47.

87 See 1 Kings 19.19–21, and the discussion of Mark 1.16–20 above.

88 Jeremias, *Parables*, p. 200.

89 R. M. Grant with D. N. Freedman, *The Secret Sayings of Jesus* (Collins Fontana 1960), p. 183.

90 Montefiore and Turner, *Thomas*, p. 59.

91 The morality of the acquisition is not the point of the parable. On arguments that the act was legitimate see J. D. Kingsbury, *The Parables of Jesus in Matthew 13* (SPCK 1969), pp. 111–12, 163.

92 Linnemann, *Parables*, pp. 101–2, 170–72; J. Dupont, 'Les Paraboles du Trésor et de la Perle', in *NTS*, 14 (1968), p. 415.

93 Cf. Kingsbury, op. cit., pp. 113, 164 who cites Jülicher, Oesterley, and Jüngel as holding this view.

94 C. H. Dodd, *The Parables of the Kingdom* (Collins Fontana 1961), pp. 84–5; R. Bultmann, *Theology of the New Testament*, I (SCM Press 1959), pp. 10–11; Percy, *Botschaft*, pp. 39–40.

95 Some react against the emphasis on 'sacrifice', and prefer to speak of a risk or stake (*Einsatz*); cf. Linnemann, *Parables*, pp. 100–105, 170–173 following Fuchs, *Studies*, pp. 94, 123–4. Linnemann is right to see allegory as read into the parables at a later stage, but may be excessively determined to avoid allegory at all costs. But her question about what precisely is demanded (p. 103) is well put.

96 Jeremias, *Parables*, p. 198; Perrin, *Teaching*, pp. 87–90, but see Kingsbury, *Parables*, p. 114, and Légasse, *L'Appel du riche*, p. 149 who are rightly cautious.

97 Kingsbury, op. cit., pp. 115–16 who is mainly interested in Matthew's use of the parables.

98 O. Glombitza, 'Der Perlenkaufmann', in *NTS*, 7 (1960–61), pp. 153–161; Légasse, op. cit., pp. 152–3 expresses some sympathy for this view, but see Dupont, 'Trésor et Perle', pp. 408, 413.

99 Fuchs, *Studies*, pp. 94–6, 123–30; see esp. p. 95.

100 Fuchs, op. cit., pp. 129–30.

101 E. Lohmeyer, *Das Evangelium des Matthäus* (Göttingen, Vandenhoeck, 1962), pp. 226–7 calls them parables for the disciples.

102 Légasse, op. cit., p. 152 for one of the parables; see also Dupont, 'Trésor et Perle', p. 416.

103 Jeremias, *Parables*, pp. 200–201 is right to emphasize this.

104 N. Cohn, *The Pursuit of the Millennium*, pp. 281–6; G. Scholem, *Sabbatai Ṣevi* (Routledge and Kegan Paul 1973), pp. 103–929; Y. Talmon, 'The Pursuit of the Millennium: The Relation between Religious and Social Change' in *European Journal of Sociology*, III (1962), pp. 125–48, partly reprinted in *Sociology and Religion* eds N. Birnbaum and G. Lenzer (Englewood Cliffs, Prentice-Hall, 1969), pp. 238–54.

105 See R. Bendix, *Max Weber* (Methuen 1966), pp. 300–302.

106 Lanternari, *Religions of the Oppressed*, pp. 247–8.

107 Cf. 1 Enoch 90.28–9; Mark 11.15–17; John 2.14–21; Mark 13.2; 14.58; 15.29; Acts 6.14. One must of course allow for embarrassment, expansion, and elaboration in the texts, but it does seem that Jesus expected the new order of things to make some difference to the Temple, to say the least. See L. Gaston, *No Stone on Another* (*Nov.T.Supp.* 23) (Leiden, Brill, 1970); R. H. Hiers, 'The Purifica-

tion of the Temple: Preparation for the Kingdom of God', in *JBL*, 90 (1971), pp. 82–90.

108 Hoehner, *Herod Antipas*, 202–24.

109 Grant, *Secret Sayings*, p. 144; Montefiore and Turner, *Thomas*, pp. 17, 96.

110 Bultmann, *Tradition*, p. 88; Manson, *Sayings*, p. 113; Degenhardt, *Lukas*, p. 85.

111 Manson, *Sayings*, p. 112; Fuchs, *Studies*, p. 106; cf. Bultmann, *Tradition*, pp. 82, 88.

112 Jeremias, *Parables*, p. 214; Légasse, *L'Appel du riche*, p. 173.

113 Fuchs, *Studies*, p. 149.

114 Degenhardt, *Lukas*, pp. 81–5; Jeremias, *Parables*, p. 215; Theissen, *Jesusbewegung*, p. 19.

115 On this question see Bultmann, op. cit., p. 104; Fuchs, op. cit., p. 107. On provision of food for birds and beasts see Job 38.41; 39.26–9; Psalm 104.27–8; 147.9.

116 Käsemann, *Essays*, p. 41.

117 Fuchs, op. cit., p. 108; cf. also Hengel, *Nachfolge*, p. 24 who cites Luke 17.6 par. See also Fuchs, op. cit., p. 160 and pp. 158–66 for some interesting but obscure comment on Jesus as proclaiming that the time for love had come.

118 E. Best, *A Commentary on the First and Second Epistles to the Thessalonians* (Black 1972), pp. 175–8, 337–41.

119 Aug. *Retr.* 21 (PL 32.638–9); cf. Légasse, op. cit., p. 172.

CHAPTER FIVE
Conclusions and Contemporary Postscript

1 J. P. Miranda, *Marx and the Bible* (SCM Press 1977), p. 19, cf. pp. 15–16; no doubt sometimes true but is it necessarily true?

2 Miranda, op. cit., p. 18.

3 Miranda, op. cit., p. 15, cf. pp. 14, 19. For a different view see N. W. Porteous, *Daniel* (SCM Press 1965), pp. 71–2.

4 G. Guttierez, *A Theology of Liberation* (SCM Press 1974), pp. 226–30; greater caution is shown by J. L. Segundo, *The Liberation of Theology* (Dublin, Gill & Macmillan, 1977), p. 111.

5 Guttierez, op. cit., pp. 297–9.

6 Especially Luke 7.22; Matthew 5.3; 16.26; Luke 16.19–31; 12.20; Matthew 25.35–6; and also 1 John 3.17, and James 2.15–16.

7 Cf. Degenhardt, *Lukas*, *passim*, and R. J. Cassidy, *Jesus, Politics and Society* (Maryknoll, NY, Orbis, 1978); also, of course, works such as J. Dupont's magisterial study, *Les Béatitudes*.

8 *Breaking Barriers, Nairobi 1975*, ed. D. M. Paton (SPCK 1976), p. 101.

9 Ibid., p. 87.

10 C. Elliott, *The Development Debate* (SCM Press 1971), pp. 82–92.

11 See the criticisms in *Christian Ethics in a Changing World*, ed. J. C. Bennett (SCM Press 1966), pp. 50–52.

12 *The Listener* (1978), pp. 602, 564. = E. Norman, *Christianity and the World Order* (Oxford University Press, 1979), pp. 19, 2.

13 *The Listener* (1978), p. 747. = Norman, op. cit., pp. 77–8.

14 G. E. M. de Ste Croix, 'Early Christian Attitudes to Property', pp. 28, 35–8. (One must admit that some later uses of Romans 13 have had disastrous results.)

15 For further discussion see R. H. Preston, 'From the Bible to the Modern World: A Problem for Ecumenical Ethics' in *BJRL* 59 (1976), pp. 164–87; D. Munby, *God and the Rich Society* (Oxford University Press 1961); D. T. Jenkins, *Equality and Excellence* (SCM Press 1961).

16 Cf. R. H. Preston, ed., *Technology and Social Justice* (SCM Press 1971), pp. 15–39, esp. pp. 34–5; B. Williams, 'The Idea of Equality', in *Philosophy, Politics and Society*, vol. 2, eds P. Laslett and W. G. Runciman (Oxford, Blackwell, 1962), pp. 110–31; J. Rawls, *A Theory of Justice* (Oxford University Press 1972); B. M. Barry, *The Liberal Theory of Justice* (Oxford, Clarendon Press, 1973); R. Nozick, *Anarchy, State and Utopia* (Oxford, Blackwell, 1975); D. Miller, *Social Justice* (Oxford, Clarendon Press, 1976), pp. 151–3, 245–9.

APPENDIX B
On *'ānî* and *'ānāw*

1 H. Graetz, *Kritischer Kommentar zu den Psalmen* (Breslau, Schottlaender, 1882) pp. 20ff.; A. Rahlfs, *'Anî und 'Anāw in den Psalmen* (Göttingen, Dieterich, 1892); I. Loeb, *La littérature des pauvres dans la Bible* (Paris, Cerf, 1892); W. W. Graf Baudissan, 'Die alttestamentliche Religion und die Armen', *Preuss. Jahrbuch*, 149 (1912), pp. 193–231; A. Causse, *Les Pauvres d'Israël* (Paris, Istra, 1922); H. Birkeland, *'Anî und 'Anāw in den Psalmen* (Oslo, Dybward, 1932–3); A. Causse, *Du Groupe ethnique à la communauté religieuse* (Paris, Alcan, 1937), pp. 243–58; A. Kuschke, 'Arm und reich im A.T. mit besonderer Berücksichtigung der nachexilischen Zeit', in *ZAW*, NF 16 (1939), pp. 31–57; J. van der Ploeg, 'Les Pauvres d'Israël et leur piété', in *Oudtestmentische Studien*, 7 (1950), pp. 236ff. A. Gelin, *Les Pauvres de Yahvé* (Paris, Cerf, 1953); E. Percy, *Die Botschaft Jesu*; H. Birkeland, *The Evildoers in the Book of Psalms* (Oslo, Dybward, 1955); S. Mowinckel, *The Psalms in Israel's Worship*, vol. 2, pp. 91–2 and 251ff.; E. Bammel, *'Ptōchos'*, *TDNT*, 6, pp. 885ff.; G. von Rad, *Theology of the Old Testament* (Edinburgh, Oliver & Boyd, 1962), 1, 400–401; H. J. Kraus, *Psalmen*, I (Neukirchen, Moers, 1960), pp. 82–3, 95.

2 Rahlfs and Driver urged the distinction with reference to the psalms, but this view is criticized in C. A. Briggs, *Psalms*, 1, ICC, (Edinburgh, Clark, 1906), p. 84, and *BDB*, p. 776.

3 Bammel, *TDNT*, 6, p. 888; E. Percy, *Botschaft*, p. 55.

4 Bammel, op. cit., 6, p. 888.

5 A. Kuschke, 'Arm und reich', pp. 50–51; cf. G. von Rad, op. cit., 1, pp. 400–401.

6 Bammel, op. cit., 6, p. 888.

7 Percy, *Botschaft*, pp. 55–63. Others (cf. *KB*[1], 720) speak of awareness before God of being poor, humble, and meek. This sounds too self-conscious. See ch. 2, n. 7 above.

8 Hauck and Schulz, *TDNT*, 6, p. 647 calculate *praüs* 8, *tapeinos* 5, *ptōchos* 4, *penēs* 4. *The preponderance of praüs* is due to the fact that it is used almost automatically as the translation of *'ānāw* in Psalms 25–149. But *penēs* is used almost equally automatically in Psalms 9–22, presumably owing to the preference of a different translator.

9 Psalms 34.3; 69.33; 22.27; and with reference to the poor in Isaiah 29.19; Amos 2.7.

10 Psalms 147.6; Proverbs 3.34 Q; 16.19 Q. The latter may be due to the pressing of the later distinction between *ānî* and *'ānāw*. See also Psalm 18.28 for the contrast of *'ānî* and the proud.

11 See K. Elliger, *Studien zum Habakuk–Kommentar vom Toten Meer* (BHT, 15) (Tübingen, Mohr, 1953), pp. 86–7, 220–22, 277; Braun, *Radikalismus*, I, 59; M. Mansoor, *The Thanksgiving Hymns* (STDJ, 3) (Leiden, Brill, 1961), pp. 49–50; 110, n. 7; Keck, 'Poor among the Saints' (1966), pp. 68–75 and Ch. 2, n. 6 above.

Index of Modern Scholars

(*Italics* indicate that a new title appears for the first time)

Index of Biblical References

(**Bold** indicates passages given some discussion)

OLD TESTAMENT

APOCRYPHA

NEW TESTAMENT